Survival Communications in Wyoming

John E. Parnell, KK4HWX

10 ISBN 1478159286
13 ISBN 978- 1478159285

Cover design by:
Lynda Colón
FREELANCE GRAPHIC DESIGN &
MARKETING COMMUNICATIONS
www.hirelynda.webs.com

I do wish to acknowledge the hard work of **Angie Shirley** in putting together the database required for this book. Without her efforts, this book could not have been done.

Titles available in this series:

Survival Communications in Alabama
Survival Communications in Alaska
Survival Communications in Arizona
Survival Communications in Arkansas
Survival Communications in California
Survival Communications in Colorado
Survival Communications in Connecticut
Survival Communications in Delaware
Survival Communications in Florida
Survival Communications in Georgia
Survival Communications in Hawaii
Survival Communications in Idaho
Survival Communications in Illinois
Survival Communications in Indiana
Survival Communications in Iowa
Survival Communications in Kansas
Survival Communications in Kentucky
Survival Communications in Louisiana
Survival Communications in Maine
Survival Communications in Maryland
Survival Communications in Massachusetts
Survival Communications in Michigan
Survival Communications in Minnesota
Survival Communications in Mississippi
Survival Communications in Missouri

Survival Communications in Montana
Survival Communications in Nebraska
Survival Communications in Nevada
Survival Communications in New Hampshire
Survival Communications in New Jersey
Survival Communications in New Mexico
Survival Communications in New York
Survival Communications in North Carolina
Survival Communications in North Dakota
Survival Communications in Ohio
Survival Communications in Oklahoma
Survival Communications in Oregon
Survival Communications in Pennsylvania
Survival Communications in Rhode Island
Survival Communications in South Carolina
Survival Communications in South Dakota
Survival Communications in Tennessee
Survival Communications in Texas
Survival Communications in Utah
Survival Communications in Vermont
Survival Communications in Virginia
Survival Communications in Washington
Survival Communications in West Virginia
Survival Communications in Wisconsin
Survival Communications in Wyoming

The above titles are available from your favorite online or brick-and-mortar bookstore or directly from the publisher at Tutor Turtle Press LLC, 1027 S. Pendleton St. – Suite B-10, Easley, SC 29642.

TABLE OF CONTENTS

Appendix A – Wyoming Ham Radio Clubs

ARRL Affiliated Amateur and Ham Radio Clubs – By City

Appendix B – Wyoming Ham Licensees by City

Survival Communications in Wyoming

Perhaps you have prepared for WTSHTF or TEOTWAWKI with respect to food, water, self-defense and shelter. But what about communication?

Whenever there is a disaster (hurricane, earthquake, economic collapse, nuclear war, EMF, solar eruption, etc.), the normal means of communication that we're all reliant upon (cell phone, land line phone, the Internet, etc.) will probably be, at best, sporadic and at worst, non-existent.

As this author sees it, short of smoke signals and mirrors, there are three options for communication in "trying times": (1) GMRS or FRS radios; (2) CB radios; and (3) ham or amateur radio. Let's consider each of these options to come up with the most acceptable one.

GMRS (General Mobile Radio Service) / FRS (Family Radio Service)

GMRS (General Mobile Radio Service) / FRS (Family Radio Service) radios work optimally over short distances where there is minimal interference. Originally designed to be used as pagers, particularly inside a building or other such confined area, these radios are low-cost and convenient to carry. Unfortunately their small size and light weight comes with a trade-off – short range and short battery life. These radios are supposed to be able to communicate for up to 25-30 miles. Right. That's on level terrain, without buildings or trees getting in the way. While battery life technology is constantly improving, you will need spare batteries to keep communicating or someway of recharging the ones in the radio. In this author's opinion, GMRS/FRS radios are not first choice when concerned with medium or long range communication.

CB (Citizens Band)

CB (Citizens Band) radios operate in a frequency range originally reserved for ham or amateur radio operation. Because of the overwhelming number of people wishing quick, low-cost, regulation-free communication, the FCC (Federal Communication Commission) split off a portion of the frequency spectrum and allowed anyone to purchase a CB radio and start communicating. No test. No license. Just personal/business communication. Today, CB radios are readily available in such outlets as eBay and Craigslist. This author has seen them at yard/garage/tag sales and at flea markets.

CB radios come in a variety of "flavors." Fixed units, sometimes referred to as base units are intended for home use. For the most part, they derive their power from the utility company. In the event of loss of electricity, most base units can also be connected to a 12-volt battery, like that in your car/truck. If you choose to obtain a fixed unit, make sure you know how to connect the unit to the battery – ahead of time. Trying to figure this out when you're under extra stress is not a good situation.

A second type of CB radio is designed to be mobile, that is, installed in your car/truck. It gets its power from the vehicle's battery. You can either attach an antenna permanently to the vehicle or have a removable, magnetic type antenna.

The third type of CB radio is designed for handheld use. They are small and light. Most weigh less than a pound and operate on batteries. Yes, using batteries in a CB poses the same limitations as those by the GMRS/FRS radios, but have the added advantage that most handheld units come with a cigarette lighter adapter. Comes in handy when you are on the move and wish to be able to communicate both from a vehicle and also when you have to abandon it.

While they have a greater range than GMRS/FRS radios, CB radios are, legally, limited to operate on 40 channels, with a power rating of four (4) watts or less. Yes, it is possible to alter CB radios to get around these limitations, but not legally,

Ham/Amateur Radio

Ham/Amateur radio is very appealing. With a ham radio, you are not limited to less than 50 miles, but can communicate with anyone in the world (who also has access to a ham radio, of course).

Standardized Amateur Radio Prepper Communications Plan

In the event of a nationwide catastrophic disaster, the nationwide network of Amateur Radio licensed preppers will need a set of standardized meeting frequencies to share information and coordinate activities between various prepper groups. This Standardized Amateur Radio Communications Plan establishes a set of frequencies on the 80 meter, 40 meter, 20 meter, and 2 meter Amateur Radio bands for use during these types of catastrophic disasters.

Routine nets will not be held on all of these frequencies, but preppers are encouraged to use them when coordinating with other preppers on a routine basis. Routine nets may be conducted by The American Preparedness Radio Net (TAPRN) on these or other frequencies as they see fit. However, TAPRN will promote the use of these standardized frequencies by all Amateur Radio licensed preppers during times of catastrophic disaster. The promotion of this Standardized Amateur Radio Communications Plan is encouraged by all means within the prepper community, including via Amateur Radio, Twitter, Facebook, and various blogs.

Standardized Frequencies and Modes
80 Meters – 3.818 MHz LSB (TAPRN Net: Sundays at 9 PM ET) 40 Meters – 7.242 MHz LSB 40 Meters Morse Code / Digital – 7.073 MHz USB (TAPRN: Sundays at 7:30 PM ET on CONTESTIA 4/250) 20 Meters – 14.242 MHz USB 2 Meters – 146.420 MHz FM

Nets and Network Etiquette

In times of nationwide catastrophic disaster, the ability of any one prepper to initiate and sustain themselves as a net control may be limited by the availability of power and other resource shortages. However, all licensed preppers are encouraged to maintain a listening watch on these frequencies as often as possible during a catastrophic disaster. Preppers may routinely announce themselves in the following manner:

• This is [Your Callsign Phonetically] in [Your State], maintaining a listening watch on [Standard Frequency] for any preppers on frequency seeking information or looking to provide information. Please call [Your Callsign Phonetically]. Preppers exchanging information that may require follow up should agree upon a designated time to return to the frequency and provide further information. If other stations are utilizing the frequency at the designated time you return, maintain watch and proceed with your communications when those stations are finished. If your communications are urgent and the stations on frequency are not passing information of a critical nature, interrupt with the word "Break" and request use of the frequency.

For More Information

Catastrophe Network: http://www.catastrophenetwork.org or @CatastropheNet on Twitter The American Preparedness Radio Network: http://www.taprn.com or @TAPRN on Twitter

© 2011 Catastrophe Network, Please Distribute Freely

In order to use a ham radio, legally, one must be licensed to do so by the FCC (other countries have analogous governmental bodies to regulate ham radio). To obtain a license is quite easy – take a test and pay your license fee. There are currently three classes of license – Technician, General, and Amateur Extra. With each of these licenses come specific abilities.

Technician class is the beginning level. The exam consists of 35 multiple choice questions randomly drawn from a pool of 395 questions. The question pool is readily available online for free downloading (http://www.ncvec.org/downloads/Revised%20Element%202.Pdf) or in such publications at *Ham Radio License Manual Revised 2nd Edition* (ISBN 978-0-87259-097-7). The current Technician pool of questions is to be used from July 1, 2010 to June 30, 2014. Be sure the question pool you are studying from is current. You will need to score at least 26 correct to pass. (Do not worry, Morse Code is no longer on the test, although many ham operators use it anyway.) You do not need to take a formal class in order to qualify to take the exam. You can learn the material on your own. Most people spend 10-15 hours studying and then successfully take the exam. The cost of taking the exam is under $20. The exam is given in MANY locations throughout the US. Usually the exam is given by area ham clubs. You do not have to belong to the club to take the exam. Check Appendix A for a listing of clubs in Wyoming.

Topics for the Technician License in Amateur Radio

The Technician license exam covers such topics as basic regulations, operating practices, and electronic theory, with a focus on VHF and UHF applications. Below is the syllabus for the Technician Class.

Subelement T1 – FCC Rules, descriptions and definitions for the amateur radio service, operator and station license responsibilities

[6 Exam Questions – 6 Groups]

T1A – Amateur Radio services; purpose of the amateur service, amateur-satellite service, operator/primary station license grant, where FCC rules are codified, basis and purpose of FCC rules, meanings of basic terms used in FCC rules

T1B – Authorized frequencies; frequency allocations, ITU regions, emission type, restricted sub-bands, spectrum sharing, transmissions near band edges

T1C – Operator classes and station call signs; operator classes, sequential, special event, and vanity call sign systems, international communications, reciprocal operation, station license licensee, places where the amateur service is regulated by the FCC, name and address on ULS, license term, renewal, grace period

T1D – Authorized and prohibited transmissions

T1E – Control operator and control types; control operator required, eligibility, designation of control operator, privileges and duties, control point, local, automatic and remote control, location of control operator

T1F – Station identification and operation standards; special operations for repeaters and auxiliary stations, third party communications, club stations, station security, FCC inspection

Subelement T2 – Operating Procedures

[3 Exam Questions – 3 Groups]

T2A – Station operation; choosing an operating frequency, calling another station, test transmissions, use of minimum power, frequency use, band plans

T2B – VHF/UHF operating practices; SSB phone, FM repeater, simplex, frequency offsets, splits and shifts, CTCSS, DTMF, tone squelch, carrier squelch, phonetics

T2C – Public service; emergency and non-emergency operations, message traffic handling

Subelement T3 – Radio wave characteristics, radio and electromagnetic properties, propagation modes

[3 Exam Questions – 3 Groups]

T3A – Radio wave characteristics; how a radio signal travels; distinctions of HF, VHF and UHF; fading, multipath; wavelength vs. penetration; antenna orientation

T3B – Radio and electromagnetic wave properties; the electromagnetic spectrum, wavelength vs. frequency, velocity of electromagnetic waves

T3C – Propagation modes; line of sight, sporadic E, meteor, aurora scatter, tropospheric ducting, F layer skip, radio horizon

Subelement T4 - Amateur radio practices and station setup

[2 Exam Questions – 2 Groups]

T4A – Station setup; microphone, speaker, headphones, filters, power source, connecting a computer, RF grounding

T4B – Operating controls; tuning, use of filters, squelch, AGC, repeater offset, memory channels

Subelement T5 – Electrical principles, math for electronics, electronic principles, Ohm's Law

[4 Exam Questions – 4 Groups]

T5A – Electrical principles; current and voltage, conductors and insulators, alternating and direct current

T5B – Math for electronics; decibels, electronic units and the metric system

T5C – Electronic principles; capacitance, inductance, current flow in circuits, alternating current, definition of RF, power calculations

T5D – Ohm's Law

Subelement T6 – Electrical components, semiconductors, circuit diagrams, component functions

[4 Exam Groups – 4 Questions]

T6A – Electrical components; fixed and variable resistors, capacitors, and inductors; fuses, switches, batteries

T6B – Semiconductors; basic principles of diodes and transistors

T6C – Circuit diagrams; schematic symbols

T6D – Component functions

Subelement T7 – Station equipment, common transmitter and receiver problems, antenna measurements and troubleshooting, basic repair and testing

[4 Exam Questions – 4 Groups]

T7A – Station radios; receivers, transmitters, transceivers

T7B – Common transmitter and receiver problems; symptoms of overload and overdrive, distortion, interference, over and under modulation, RF feedback, off frequency signals; fading and noise; problems with digital communications interfaces

T7C – Antenna measurements and troubleshooting; measuring SWR, dummy loads, feedline failure modes

T7D – Basic repair and testing; soldering, use of a voltmeter, ammeter, and ohmmeter

Subelement T8 – Modulation modes, amateur satellite operation, operating activities, non-voice communications

[4 Exam Questions – 4 Groups]

T8A – Modulation modes; bandwidth of various signals

T8B – Amateur satellite operation; Doppler shift, basic orbits, operating protocols

T8C – Operating activities; radio direction finding, radio control, contests, special event stations, basic linking over Internet

T8D – Non-voice communications; image data, digital modes, CW, packet, PSK31

Subelement T9 – Antennas, feedlines

[2 Exam Groups – 2 Questions]

T9A – Antennas; vertical and horizontal, concept of gain, common portable and mobile antennas, relationships between antenna length and frequency

T9B – Feedlines; types, losses vs. frequency, SWR concepts, matching, weather protection, connectors

Subelement T0 – AC power circuits, antenna installation, RF hazards

[3 Exam Questions – 3 Groups]

T0A – AC power circuits; hazardous voltages, fuses and circuit breakers, grounding, lightning protection, battery safety, electrical code compliance

T0B – Antenna installation; tower safety, overhead power lines

T0C – RF hazards; radiation exposure, proximity to antennas, recognized safe power levels, exposure to others

Once your name and call sign are available in the FCC database, you have the privilege of operating on all VHF (2 m) and UHF (70 cm) frequencies above 30 megahertz (MHz) and HF frequencies 80, 40, and 15 meter, and on the 10 meter band using Morse code (CW), voice, and digital mode. For a Technician license in Wyoming, your call sign will consist of a two-letter prefix beginning with K or W, the number seven (7), and a three-letter suffix. The single digit number in the call sign is determined according to which area of the US you obtain your first license. Even though you may move to another state, you keep this number in your call sign. This is also true should you upgrade to a higher license and get a new call sign. The numeral portion of your call sign stays the same.

Call Sign Numbers

Below is a chart showing the various numbers and the state(s) in which you would obtain the number.

Call Sign Number	State(s)
0	CO, IA, KS, MN, MO, NE, ND, SD
1	CT, ME, MA, NH, RI, VT
2	NJ, NY
3	DE, DC, MD, PA
4	AL, FL, GA, KY, NC, SC, TN, VA
5	AR, LA, MS, NM, OK, TX
6	CA
7	AZ, ID, MT, NV, OR, WA, UT, WY
8	MI, OH, WV
9	IL, IN, WI

Residents of Alaska may have any of the following call sign prefixes assigned to them: AL0-7, KL0-7, NL0-7, or WL0-7. Likewise, residents of Hawaii may have the prefix AH6-7, KH6-7, NH6-7, or WH6-7 assigned.

Once you obtain your Technician license, do not stop there. Go and get your General license.

General is the second of three ham license classes. Like the Technician license, to get a General license, you merely have to take a 35-question multiple choice exam and pay your license fee. Passing is still at least 26 correct answers and the fee is the same (less than $20). Again the question pool is available for free online (http://www.ncvec.org/page.php?id=358). It is also available in such print publications as *The ARRL General Class License Manual 7th Edition* (ISBN 978-0-87259-811-9). The current General pool of questions is to be used from July 1, 2011 to June 30, 2015. Be sure the question pool you are using is current. Being a bit more comprehensive than the Technician license, the General license usually requires 15-20 hours of study to learn the material. Check Appendix A for a listing of clubs in Wyoming where you might take your exam. Once your name and NEW call sign is listed in the FCC database, you're good to go. For a General license in Wyoming, your call sign will consist of a one-letter prefix beginning with K, N or W, the number seven (7), and a three-letter suffix.

Topics for the General License in Amateur Radio

The General license exam covers regulations, operating practices and electronic theory. Below is the syllabus for the General Class.

Subelement G1 – Commission's Rules
(5 Exam Questions – 5 Groups)
G1A – General Class control operator frequency privileges; primary and secondary allocations
G1B – Antenna structure limitations; good engineering and good amateur practice, beacon operation; restricted operation; retransmitting radio signals
G1C – Transmitter power regulations; data emission standards
G1D – Volunteer Examiners and Volunteer Examiner Coordinators; temporary identification
G1E – Control categories; repeater regulations; harmful interference; third party rules; ITU regions

Subelement G2 – Operating procedures
(5 Exam Questions – 5 Groups)
G2A – Phone operating procedures; USB/LSB utilization conventions; procedural signals; breaking into a OSO in progress; VOX operation
G2B – Operating courtesy; band plans, emergencies, including drills and emergency communications
G2C – CW operating procedures and procedural signals; Q signals and common abbreviations; full break in
G2D – Amateur Auxiliary; minimizing interference; HF operations

G2E – Digital operating; procedures, procedural signals and common abbreviations

Subelement G3 – Radio wave propagation

(3 Exam Questions – 3 Groups)

G3A – Sunspots and solar radiation; ionospheric disturbances; propagation forecasting and indices

G3B – Maximum Usable Frequency; Lowest Usable Frequency; propagation

G3C – Ionospheric layers; critical angle and frequency; HF scatter; Near Vertical Incidence Sky waves

Subelement G4 – Amateur radio practices

(5 Exam Questions – 5 Groups)

G4A – Station Operation and setup

G4B – Test and monitoring equipment; two-tone test

G4C – Interference with consumer electronics; grounding; DSP

G4D – Speech processors; S meters; sideband operation near band edges

G4E – HF mobile radio installations; emergency and battery powered operation

Subelement G5 – Electrical principles

(3 Exam Questions – 3 Groups)

G5A – Reactance; inductance; capacitance; impedance; impedance matching

G5B – The Decibel; current and voltage dividers; electrical power calculations; sine wave root-mean-square (RMS) values; PEP calculations

G5C – Resistors; capacitors and inductors in series and parallel; transformers

Subelement G6 – Circuit components

(3 Exam Questions – 3 Groups)

G6A – Resistors; capacitors; inductors

G6B – Rectifiers; solid state diodes and transistors; vacuum tubes; batteries

G6C – Analog and digital integrated circuits (ICs); microprocessors; memory; I/O devices; microwave ICs (MMICs); display devices

Subelement G7 – Practical circuits

(3 Exam Questions – 3 Groups)

G7A – Power supplies; schematic symbols

G7B – Digital circuits; amplifiers and oscillators

G7C – Receivers and transmitters; filters, oscillators

Subelement G8 – Signals and emissions

(2 Exam Questions – 2 Groups)

G8A – Carriers and modulation; AM; FM; single and double sideband; modulation envelope; overmodulation
G8B – Frequency mixing; multiplication; HF data communications; bandwidths of various modes; deviation

Subelement G9 – Antennas and feed lines

(4 Exam Questions – 4 Groups)
G9A – Antenna feed lines; characteristic impedance and attenuation; SWR calculation, measurement and effects; matching networks
G9B – Basic antennas
G9C – Directional antennas
G9D – Specialized antennas

Subelement G0 – Electrical and RF safety

(2 Exam Questions – 2 Groups)
G0A – RF safety principles, rules and guidelines; routine station elevation
G0B – Safety in the ham shack; electrical shock and treatment, safety grounding, fusing, interlocks, wiring, antenna and tower safety

With a General license, you can use all VHF and UHF frequencies and most of the HF frequencies. You would have access to the 160, 30, 17, 12, and 10 meter bands and access to major parts of the 80, 40, 20, and 15 meter bands. Of course, this is in addition to all bands available to Technician license holders.

Amateur Extra is the third of three ham license classes. Like the Technician and General classes, you merely have to pass a test and pay your fee to get your Amateur Extra license. This class of license is more comprehensive than the lower license classes. The exam is longer – 50 questions – and the minimum passing score is higher – 37. However, once you get your Amateur Extra license, all ham frequencies, VHF, UHF and HF are available for your enjoyment. The Extra exam covers regulations, specialized operating practices, advanced electronics theory, and radio equipment design.

Like for the other license classes, the question pool for the Amateur Extra license is available online for downloading (http://www.ncvec.org/downloads/REVISED%202012-2016%20Extra%20Class%20Pool.doc). It is also available in print form in such publications as *The ARRL Extra Class License Manual Revised 9th Edition* (ISBN 978-0-87259-887-4).

Topics for the Extra License in Amateur Radio

Below is the syllabus for the Amateur Extra Class for July 1, 2012 to June 30, 2016.

Subelement E1 – Commission's Rules

[6 Exam Questions – 6 Groups]
E1A – Operating Standards: frequency privileges; emission standards; automatic message forwarding; frequency sharing; stations aboard ships or aircraft

E1B – Station restrictions and special operations: restrictions on station location; general operating restrictions, spurious emissions, control operator reimbursement; antenna structure restrictions; RACES operations

E1C – Station control: definitions and restrictions pertaining to local, automatic and remote control operation; control operator responsibilities for remote and automatically controlled stations

E1D – Amateur Satellite service: definitions and purpose; license requirements for space stations; available frequencies and bands; telecommand and telemetry operations; restrictions, and special provisions; notification requirements

E1E – Volunteer examiner program: definitions, qualifications, preparation and administration of exams; accreditation; question pools; documentation requirements

E1F – Miscellaneous rules: external RF power amplifiers; national quiet zone; business communications; compensated communications; spread spectrum; auxiliary stations; reciprocal operating privileges; IARP and CEPT licenses; third party communications with foreign countries; special temporary authority

Subelement E2 – Operating procedures

[5 Exam Questions – 5 Groups]

E2A – Amateur radio in space: amateur satellites; orbital mechanics; frequencies and modes; satellite hardware; satellite operations

E2B – Television practices: fast scan television standards and techniques; slow scan television standards and techniques

E2C – Operating methods: contest and DX operating; spread-spectrum transmissions; selecting an operating frequency

E2D – Operating methods: VHF and UHF digital modes; APRS

E2E – Operating methods: operating HF digital modes; error correction

Subelement E3 – Radio wave propagation

[3 Exam Questions – 3 Groups]

E3A – Propagation and technique, Earth-Moon-Earth communications; meteor scatter

E3B – Propagation and technique, trans-equatorial; long path; gray-line; multi-path propagation

E3C – Propagation and technique, Aurora propagation; selective fading; radio-path horizon; take-off angle over flat or sloping terrain; effects of ground on propagation; less common propagation modes

Subelement E4 – Amateur practices

[5 Exam Questions – 5 Groups]

E4A – Test equipment: analog and digital instruments; spectrum and network analyzers, antenna analyzers; oscilloscopes; testing transistors; RF measurements

E4B – Measurement technique and limitations: instrument accuracy and performance limitations; probes; techniques to minimize errors; measurement of "Q"; instrument calibration

E4C – Receiver performance characteristics, phase noise, capture effect, noise floor, image rejection, MDS, signal-to-noise-ratio; selectivity

E4D – Receiver performance characteristics, blocking dynamic range, intermodulation and cross-modulation interference; 3rd order intercept; desensitization; preselection

E4E – Noise suppression: system noise; electrical appliance noise; line noise; locating noise sources; DSP noise reduction; noise blankers

Subelement E5 – Electrical principles

[4 Exam Questions – 4 Groups]

E5A – Resonance and Q: characteristics of resonant circuits: series and parallel resonance; Q; half-power bandwidth; phase relationships in reactive circuits

E5B – Time constants and phase relationships: RLC time constants: definition; time constants in RL and RC circuits; phase angle between voltage and current; phase angles of series and parallel circuits

E5C – Impedance plots and coordinate systems: plotting impedances in polar coordinates; rectangular coordinates

E5D – AC and RF energy in real circuits: skin effect; electrostatic and electromagnetic fields; reactive power; power factor; coordinate systems

Subelement E6 – Circuit components

[6 Exam Questions – 6 Groups]

E6A – Semiconductor materials and devices: semiconductor materials germanium, silicon, P-type, N-type; transistor types: NPN, PNP, junction, field-effect transistors: enhancement mode; depletion mode; MOS; CMOS; N-channel; P-channel

E6B – Semiconductor diodes

E6C – Integrated circuits: TTL digital integrated circuits; CMOS digital integrated circuits; gates

E6D – Optical devices and toroids: cathode-ray tube devices; charge-coupled devices (CCDs); liquid crystal displays (LCDs); toroids: permeability, core material, selecting, winding

E6E – Piezoelectric crystals and MMICs: quartz crystals; crystal oscillators and filters; monolithic amplifiers

E6F – Optical components and power systems: photoconductive principles and effects, photovoltaic systems, optical couplers, optical sensors, and optoisolators

Subelement E7 – Practical circuits

[8 Exam Questions – 8 Groups]

E7A – Digital circuits: digital circuit principles and logic circuits: classes of logic elements; positive and negative logic; frequency dividers; truth tables

E7B – Amplifiers: Class of operation; vacuum tube and solid-state circuits; distortion and intermodulation; spurious and parasitic suppression; microwave amplifiers

E7C – Filters and matching networks: filters and impedance matching networks: types of networks; types of filters; filter applications; filter characteristics; impedance matching; DSP filtering

E7D – Power supplies and voltage regulators

E7E – Modulation and demodulation: reactance, phase and balanced modulators; detectors; mixer stages; DSP modulation and demodulation; software defined radio systems

E7F – Frequency markers and counters: frequency divider circuits; frequency marker generators; frequency counters

E7G – Active filters and op-amps: active audio filters; characteristics; basic circuit design; operational amplifiers

E7H – Oscillators and signal sources: types of oscillators; synthesizers and phase-locked loops; direct digital synthesizers

Subelement E8 – Signals and emissions

[4 Exam Questions – 4 Groups]

E8A – AC waveforms: sine, square, sawtooth and irregular waveforms; AC measurements; average and PEP of RF signals; pulse and digital signal waveforms

E8B – Modulation and demodulation: modulation methods; modulation index and deviation ratio; pulse modulation; frequency and time division multiplexing

E8C – Digital signals: digital communications modes; CW; information rate vs. bandwidth; spread-spectrum communications; modulation methods

E8D – Waves, measurements, and RF grounding: peak-to-peak values, polarization; RF grounding

Subelement E9 – Antennas and transmission lines

[8 Exam Questions – 8 Groups]

E9A – Isotropic and gain antennas: definition; used as a standard for comparison; radiation pattern; basic antenna parameters: radiation resistance and reactance, gain, beamwidth, efficiency

E9B – Antenna patterns: E and H plane patterns; gain as a function of pattern; antenna design; Yagi antennas

E9C – Wire and phased vertical antennas: beverage antennas; terminated and resonant rhombic antennas; elevation above real ground; ground effects as related to polarization; take-off angles

E9D – Directional antennas: gain; satellite antennas; antenna beamwidth; losses; SWR bandwidth; antenna efficiency; shortened and mobile antennas; grounding

E9E – Matching: matching antennas to feed lines; power dividers

E9F – Transmission lines: characteristics of open and shorted feed lines: 1/8 wavelength; 1/4 wavelength; 1/2 wavelength; feed lines: coax versus open-wire; velocity factor; electrical length; transformation characteristics of line terminated in impedance not equal to characteristic impedance

E9G – The Smith chart

E9H – Effective radiated power; system gains and losses; radio direction finding antennas

Subelement E0 – Safety

[1 exam question – 1 group]

E0A – Safety: amateur radio safety practices; RF radiation hazards; hazardous materials

Once your new call sign is listed in the FCC database, you are good to go. For an Amateur Extra license in Wyoming, your call sign will consist of a prefix of K, N or W, the number seven (7), and a two-letter suffix, or a two-letter prefix beginning with A, N, K or W, the number seven (7), and a one-letter suffix, or a two-letter prefix beginning with A, the number seven (7), and a two-letter suffix.

Ham radio equipment can be expensive or you can do it "on the cheap." The cost will run from a couple hundred dollars to well in the thousands, depending on what you have available. eBay, and Craigslist are good places to start looking. Most ham clubs do some sort of hamfest annually wherein club members or others are willing to part with older equipment. See Appendix A for a list of clubs in Wyoming.

Another excellent source of equipment, as well as advice on setting the equipment up and how to use it properly, is current ham operators. In Appendix B, the author has listed all the FCC licensed ham operators in Wyoming, listed by city, and then sorted by street and house number on the street. Who knows, maybe someone who lives close to you is a ham operator. Be a good neighbor, stop by and have a chat with him/her.

Like CB radios, ham radios come in three formats – base, mobile, and handheld. They can use the electric company for power, or operate off a car battery. In the opinion of this author, in spite of the slightly higher cost of the equipment and having to take a test to legally use the equipment, ham radio is the way to go when concerned about communication during times of crisis.

Canadian Call Sign Prefixes

Because of our proximity to Canada, many times ham contact is made with our northern neighbors. Below is a chart showing the origin of Canadian call sign prefixes.

Call Sign Prefix	Provence or Territory
CY0	Sable Island
CY9	St. Paul Island
VA1, VE1	New Brunswick, Nova Scotia
VA2, VE2	Quebec
VA3, VE3	Ontario
VA4, VE4	Manitoba
VA5, VE5	Saskatchewan
VA6, VE6	Alberta
VA7, VE7	British Columbia
VE8	North West Territories
VE9	New Brunswick
VO1	Newfoundland
VO2	Labrador
VY0	Nunavut
VY1	Yukon
VY2	Prince Edward Island

Common Radio Bands in the United States

Certain radio bands are more popular with ham radio enthusiasts than others. Below is a chart showing these bands and when they are most popular.

	Band (meter)	Frequency (MHz)	Use
HF	160	1.8 – 2.0	Night
	80	3.5 – 4.0	Night and Local Day
	40	7.0 – 7.3	Night and Local Day
	30	10.1 – 10.15	CW and Digital
	20	14.0 – 14.350	World Wide Day and Night
	17	18.068 – 18.168	World Wide Day and Night
	15	21.0 – 21.450	Primarily Daytime
	12	24.890 – 24.990	Primarily Daytime
	10	28.0 – 29.70	Daytime during Sunspot highs
VHF	6	50 – 54	Local to World Wide
	2	144 – 148	Local to Medium Distance
UHF	70 cm	430 – 440	Local

Common Amateur Radio Bands in Canada

160 Meter Band - Maximum bandwidth 6 kHz

1.800 - 1.820 MHz - CW
1.820 - 1.830 MHz - Digital Modes
1 830 - 1.840 MHz - DX Window
1.840 - 2.000 MHz - SSB and other wide band modes

80 Meter Band - Maximum bandwidth 6 kHz

3.500 - 3.580 MHz - CW
3.580 - 3.620 MHz - Digital Modes
3.620 - 3.635 MHz - Packet/Digital Secondary
3.635 - 3.725 MHz - CW
3.725 - 3.790 MHz - SSB and other side band modes*
3.790 - 3.800 MHz - SSB DX Window
3.800 - 4.000 MHz - SSB and other wide band modes

40 Meter Band - Maximum bandwidth 6 kHz

7.000 - 7.035 MHz - CW
7.035 - 7.050 MHz - Digital Modes
7.040 - 7.050 MHz - International packet
7.050 - 7.100 MHz - SSB
7.100 - 7.120 MHz - Packet within Region 2
7.120 - 7.150 MHz - CW
7.150 - 7.300 MHz - SSB and other wide band modes

30 Meter Band - Maximum bandwidth 1 kHz

10.100 - 10.130 MHz - CW only
10.130 - 10.140 MHz - Digital Modes
10.140 - 10.150 MHz - Packet

20 Meter Band - Maximum bandwidth 6 kHz

14.000 - 14.070 MHz - CW only
14.070 - 14.095 MHz - Digital Mode
14.095 - 14.099 MHz - Packet
14.100 MHz - Beacons
14.101 - 14.112 MHz - CW, SSB, packet shared
14.112 - 14.350 MHz - SSB
14.225 - 14.235 MHz - SSTV

17 Meter Band - Maximum bandwidth 6 kHz

18.068 - 18.100 MHz - CW
18.100 - 18.105 MHz - Digital Modes
18.105 - 18.110 MHz - Packet
18.110 - 18.168 MHz - SSB and other wide band modes

15 Meter Band - maximum bandwidth 6 kHz

21.000 - 21.070 MHz - CW
21.070 - 21.090 MHz - Digital Modes
21.090 - 21.125 MHz - Packet
21.100 - 21.150 MHz - CW and SSB
21.150 - 21.335 MHz - SSB and other wide band modes
21.335 - 21.345 MHz - SSTV
21.345 - 21.450 MHz - SSB and other wide band modes

12 Meter Band - Maximum bandwidth 6 kHz

24.890 - 24.930 MHz - CW
24.920 - 24.925 MHz - Digital Modes
24.925 - 24.930 MHz - Packet
24.930 - 24.990 MHz - SSB and other wide band modes

10 Meter Band - Maximum band width 20 kHz

28.000 - 28.200 MHz - CW
28.070 - 28.120 MHz - Digital Modes
28.120 - 28.190 MHz - Packet
28.190 - 28.200 MHz - Beacons
28.200 - 29.300 MHz - SSB and other wide band modes
29.300 - 29.510 MHz - Satellite
29.510 - 29.700 MHz - SSB, FM and repeaters

160 Meters (1.8-2.0 MHz)

1.800 - 2.000 CW
1.800 - 1.810 Digital Modes
1.810 CW QRP
1.843-2.000 SSB, SSTV and other wideband modes
1.910 SSB QRP
1.995 - 2.000 Experimental
1.999 - 2.000 Beacons

80 Meters (3.5-4.0 MHz)

3.590 RTTY/Data DX
3.570-3.600 RTTY/Data
3.790-3.800 DX window
3.845 SSTV
3.885 AM calling frequency

40 Meters (7.0-7.3 MHz)

7.040 RTTY/Data DX
7.080-7.125 RTTY/Data
7.171 SSTV
7.290 AM calling frequency

30 Meters (10.1-10.15 MHz)

10.130-10.140 RTTY
10.140-10.150 Packet

20 Meters (14.0-14.35 MHz)

14.070-14.095 RTTY
14.095-14.0995 Packet
14.100 NCDXF Beacons
14.1005-14.112 Packet
14.230 SSTV
14.286 AM calling frequency

17 Meters (18.068-18.168 MHz)

18.100-18.105 RTTY
18.105-18.110 Packet

15 Meters (21.0-21.45 MHz)

21.070-21.110 RTTY/Data
21.340 SSTV

12 Meters (24.89-24.99 MHz)

24.920-24.925 RTTY
24.925-24.930 Packet

10 Meters (28-29.7 MHz)

28.000-28.070 CW
28.070-28.150 RTTY
28.150-28.190 CW
28.200-28.300 Beacons
28.300-29.300 Phone
28.680 SSTV
29.000-29.200 AM
29.300-29.510 Satellite Downlinks
29.520-29.590 Repeater Inputs
29.600 FM Simplex
29.610-29.700 Repeater Outputs

6 Meters (50-54 MHz)

50.0-50.1 CW, beacons
50.060-50.080 beacon subband
50.1-50.3 SSB, CW
50.10-50.125 DX window
50.125 SSB calling
50.3-50.6 All modes
50.6-50.8 Nonvoice communications
50.62 Digital (packet) calling
50.8-51.0 Radio remote control (20-kHz channels)
51.0-51.1 Pacific DX window
51.12-51.48 Repeater inputs (19 channels)
51.12-51.18 Digital repeater inputs
51.5-51.6 Simplex (six channels)
51.62-51.98 Repeater outputs (19 channels)
51.62-51.68 Digital repeater outputs
52.0-52.48 Repeater inputs (except as noted; 23 channels)
52.02, 52.04 FM simplex
52.2 TEST PAIR (input)
52.5-52.98 Repeater output (except as noted; 23 channels)
52.525 Primary FM simplex
52.54 Secondary FM simplex
52.7 TEST PAIR (output)
53.0-53.48 Repeater inputs (except as noted; 19 channels)
53.0 Remote base FM simplex
53.02 Simplex
53.1, 53.2, 53.3, 53.4 Radio remote control
53.5-53.98 Repeater outputs (except as noted; 19 channels)
53.5, 53.6, 53.7, 53.8 Radio remote control
53.52, 53.9 Simplex

2 Meters (144-148 MHz)

144.00-144.05 EME (CW)
144.05-144.10 General CW and weak signals
144.10-144.20 EME and weak-signal SSB
144.200 National calling frequency
144.200-144.275 General SSB operation
144.275-144.300 Propagation beacons
144.30-144.50 New OSCAR subband
144.50-144.60 Linear translator inputs
144.60-144.90 FM repeater inputs
144.90-145.10 Weak signal and FM simplex (145.01,03,05,07,09 are widely used for packet)
145.10-145.20 Linear translator outputs
145.20-145.50 FM repeater outputs
145.50-145.80 Miscellaneous and experimental modes
145.80-146.00 OSCAR subband
146.01-146.37 Repeater inputs
146.40-146.58 Simplex
146.52 National Simplex Calling Frequency
146.61-146.97 Repeater outputs
147.00-147.39 Repeater outputs
147.42-147.57 Simplex
147.60-147.99 Repeater inputs

1.25 Meters (222-225 MHz)

222.0-222.150 Weak-signal modes
222.0-222.025 EME
222.05-222.06 Propagation beacons
222.1 SSB & CW calling frequency
222.10-222.15 Weak-signal CW & SSB
222.15-222.25 Local coordinator's option; weak signal, ACSB, repeater inputs, control
222.25-223.38 FM repeater inputs only
223.40-223.52 FM simplex
223.52-223.64 Digital, packet
223.64-223.70 Links, control
223.71-223.85 Local coordinator's option; FM simplex, packet, repeater outputs
223.85-224.98 Repeater outputs only

70 Centimeters (420-450 MHz)

420.00-426.00 ATV repeater or simplex with 421.25 MHz video carrier control links and experimental
426.00-432.00 ATV simplex with 427.250-MHz video carrier frequency
432.00-432.07 EME (Earth-Moon-Earth)
432.07-432.10 Weak-signal CW
432.10 70-cm calling frequency

432.10-432.30 Mixed-mode and weak-signal work
432.30-432.40 Propagation beacons
432.40-433.00 Mixed-mode and weak-signal work
433.00-435.00 Auxiliary/repeater links
435.00-438.00 Satellite only (internationally)
438.00-444.00 ATV repeater input with 439.250-MHz video carrier frequency and repeater links
442.00-445.00 Repeater inputs and outputs (local option)
445.00-447.00 Shared by auxiliary and control links, repeaters and simplex (local option)
446.00 National simplex frequency
447.00-450.00 Repeater inputs and outputs (local option)

33 Centimeters (902-928 MHz)

902.0-903.0 Narrow-bandwidth, weak-signal communications
902.0-902.8 SSTV, FAX, ACSSB, experimental
902.1 Weak-signal calling frequency
902.8-903.0 Reserved for EME, CW expansion
903.1 Alternate calling frequency
903.0-906.0 Digital communications
906-909 FM repeater inputs
909-915 ATV
915-918 Digital communications
918-921 FM repeater outputs
921-927 ATV
927-928 FM simplex and links

23 Centimeters (1240-1300 MHz)

1240-1246 ATV #1
1246-1248 Narrow-bandwidth FM point-to-point links and digital, duplex with 1258-1260.
1248-1258 Digital Communications
1252-1258 ATV #2
1258-1260 Narrow-bandwidth FM point-to-point links digital, duplexed with 1246-1252
1260-1270 Satellite uplinks, reference WARC '79
1260-1270 Wide-bandwidth experimental, simplex ATV
1270-1276 Repeater inputs, FM and linear, paired with 1282-1288, 239 pairs every 25 kHz, e.g. 1270.025, .050, etc.
1271-1283 Non-coordinated test pair
1276-1282 ATV #3
1282-1288 Repeater outputs, paired with 1270-1276
1288-1294 Wide-bandwidth experimental, simplex ATV
1294-1295 Narrow-bandwidth FM simplex services, 25-kHz channels
1294.5 National FM simplex calling frequency
1295-1297 Narrow bandwidth weak-signal communications (no FM)
1295.0-1295.8 SSTV, FAX, ACSSB, experimental
1295.8-1296.0 Reserved for EME, CW expansion

1296.00-1296.05 EME-exclusive
1296.07-1296.08 CW beacons
1296.1 CW, SSB calling frequency
1296.4-1296.6 Crossband linear translator input
1296.6-1296.8 Crossband linear translator output
1296.8-1297.0 Experimental beacons (exclusive)
1297-1300 Digital Communications

2300-2310 and 2390-2450 MHz

2300.0-2303.0 High-rate data
2303.0-2303.5 Packet
2303.5-2303.8 TTY packet
2303.9-2303.9 Packet, TTY, CW, EME
2303.9-2304.1 CW, EME
2304.1 Calling frequency
2304.1-2304.2 CW, EME, SSB
2304.2-2304.3 SSB, SSTV, FAX, Packet AM, Amtor
2304.30-2304.32 Propagation beacon network
2304.32-2304.40 General propagation beacons
2304.4-2304.5 SSB, SSTV, ACSSB, FAX, Packet AM, Amtor experimental
2304.5-2304.7 Crossband linear translator input
2304.7-2304.9 Crossband linear translator output
2304.9-2305.0 Experimental beacons
2305.0-2305.2 FM simplex (25 kHz spacing)
2305.20 FM simplex calling frequency
2305.2-2306.0 FM simplex (25 kHz spacing)
2306.0-2309.0 FM Repeaters (25 kHz) input
2309.0-2310.0 Control and auxiliary links
2390.0-2396.0 Fast-scan TV
2396.0-2399.0 High-rate data
2399.0-2399.5 Packet
2399.5-2400.0 Control and auxiliary links
2400.0-2403.0 Satellite
2403.0-2408.0 Satellite high-rate data
2408.0-2410.0 Satellite
2410.0-2413.0 FM repeaters (25 kHz) output
2413.0-2418.0 High-rate data
2418.0-2430.0 Fast-scan TV
2430.0-2433.0 Satellite
2433.0-2438.0 Satellite high-rate data
2438.0-2450.0 WB FM, FSTV, FMTV, SS experimental

3300-3500 MHz

3456.3-3456.4 Propagation beacons

5650-5925 MHz
5760.3-5760.4 Propagation beacons

10.00-10.50 GHz
10.368 Narrow band calling frequency 10.3683-10.3684 Propagation beacons 10.3640 Calling frequency

Now that you have your license (you do, don't you?), and your equipment, you are ready to go live. Below is a suggested start.

1) Assuming you have the HT set up to the appropriate frequency, and offset, press the mic button on the HT and say, "KK4HWX listening." Replace the KK4HWX with your own call sign, the one assigned to you by the FCC (it's the law). If no one responds to your call, you may wish to try again. Hopefully someone will respond to your call.

2) Once you get a response, it will be in the form of something like, "KK4HWX this is ??1??? in Eastport returning. My name is Florence. Back to you. ??1???" then a tone. Let us examine the response more closely. She first acknowledged your call sign (KK4HWX), then identified hers (??1???). From the 1 in her call sign, you know that she first got her license in Region 1, meaning she got it while a resident of CT, ME, MA, NH, RI, or VT. She then told you where she's transmitting from (Eastport). The term "returning" means that she is returning your call. Her name is Florence. The phrase, "Back to you" indicates that she is turning over the conversation to you. She then repeats her call sign. The tone indicates to you that it is okay to proceed with your response. BTW if she had used the term "Over" instead of "Back to you," it would mean the same thing, just fewer words.

3) At this point, press the mic button and continue with the conversation. You should restate your call sign often during the conversation (perhaps every 10 minutes or less and whenever you begin transmitting). Don't forget to say, "Over" or "Back to you" whenever you are giving Florence control of the conversation again.

4) When you are ready to stop the conversation, you should say goodbye or use the phrase "73", meaning "best wishes." Your conversation would end something like, "??1??? 73, this is KK4HWX clear and monitoring." The "clear and monitoring" indicates that you are going to continue to monitor the frequency. If you are not going to continue monitoring, you may wish to end the conversation with Florence with, "clear and QRT" instead. The QRT means that you are stopping transmissions.

Call Sign Phonics

Because of different accents of various people, sometimes it is difficult to understand call sign letters when spoken. For this reason, most ham operators verbalize their call sign using phonics. Below is a table listing the accepted phonics for letters and numbers.

A = ALFA	S = SIERRA
B = BRAVO	T = TANGO
C = CHARLIE	U = UNIFORM
D = DELTA	V = VICTOR
E = ECHO	W = WHISKEY
F = FOXTROT	X = X-RAY
G = GOLF	Y = YANKEE
H = HOTEL	Z = ZULU (ZED)
I = INDIA	1 = ONE
J = JULIETT	2 = TWO
K = KILO	3 = THREE (TREE)
L = LIMA	4 = FOUR
M = MIKE	5 = FIVE (FIFE)
N = NOVEMBER	6 = SIX
O = OSCAR	7 = SEVEN
P = PAPA (PA-PA')	8 = EIGHT
Q = QUEBEC (KAY-BEK')	9 = NINE (NINER)
R = ROMEO	0 = ZERO

The words in parentheses are the pronunciation or the alternate pronunciations for the words or numbers, but you will hear both used. With the letter Z, (ZED) is by far the most commonly used. With the number 9, NINER is the most common and easiest to understand ON THE AIR.

If you wish to use Morse code (CW) instead of voice communication, the "conversation" would follow the same steps, with a few modifications. To type out each word would require a lot of typing and translating. If you are like this author, more means more, i.e., more typing means more typos are likely. To help with this situation, CW enthusiasts have developed a language all their own – they use abbreviations for common phrases. Below is a chart showing some of these abbreviations.

Abbreviation	Use
AR	Over
de	From or "this is"
ES	And
GM	Good Morning
K	Go
KN	Go only
NM	Name
QTH	Location
RPT	Report
R	Roger
SK	Clear
tnx	Thanks
UR	Your, you are
73	Best Wishes

Morse Code and Amateur Radio

If you wish to use CW, but are concerned about accuracy, you might consider purchasing a Morse code translator. This is an electronic device that you place in front of your speakers. It takes the CW sounds and translates them into English and displays the transmission on an LCD display. For the reverse, you can pick up a CW keyboard. With the keyboard, you type in your message and it converts the text to Morse code. The translator does not need to be attached to your ham equipment, whereas the keyboard would.

For your convenience, below is a table showing the Morse code signals and their meaning.

Character	Code
A	· —
B	— · · ·
C	— · — ·
D	— · ·
E	·
F	· · — ·
G	— — ·
H	· · · ·
I	· ·
J	· — — —
K	— · —
L	· — · ·
M	— —
N	— ·
O	— — —
P	· — — ·
Q	— — · —
R	· — ·
S	· · ·
T	—
U	· · —
V	· · · —
W	· — —
X	— · · —
Y	— · — —
Z	— — · ·
0	— — — — —
1	· — — — —
2	· · — — —
3	· · · — —
4	· · · · —
5	· · · · ·

6	— · · · ·
7	— — · · ·
8	— — — · ·
9	— — — — ·
Ampersand [&], Wait	· — · · ·
Apostrophe [']	· — — — — ·
At sign [@]	· — — · — ·
Colon [:]	— — — · · ·
Comma [,]	— — · · — —
Dollar sign [$]	· · · — · · —
Double dash [=]	— · · · —
Exclamation mark [!]	— · — · — —
Hyphen, Minus [-]	— · · · · —
Parenthesis closed [)]	— · — — · —
Parenthesis open [(]	— · — — ·
Period [.]	· — · — · —
Plus [+]	· — · — ·
Question mark [?]	· · — — · ·
Quotation mark ["]	· — · · — ·
Semicolon [;]	— · — · — ·
Slash [/], Fraction bar	— · · — ·
Underscore [_]	· · — — · —

An advantage of using Morse Code is that when broadcasting CW, you are using reduced power, thereby saving your battery. Your battery is used only while actually transmitting or receiving.

International Call Sign Prefixes

As was stated earlier, all ham radio call signs begin with letters (or numbers) taken from blocks assigned to each country of the world by the *ITU - International Telecommunications Union,* a body controlled by the United Nations. The following chart indicates which call sign series are allocated to which countries.

Call Sign Series	Allocated to
AAA-ALZ	**United States of America**
AMA-AOZ	Spain
APA-ASZ	Pakistan (Islamic Republic of)
ATA-AWZ	India (Republic of)
AXA-AXZ	Australia
AYA-AZZ	Argentine Republic
A2A-A2Z	Botswana (Republic of)
A3A-A3Z	Tonga (Kingdom of)
A4A-A4Z	Oman (Sultanate of)
A5A-A5Z	Bhutan (Kingdom of)

A6A-A6Z	United Arab Emirates
A7A-A7Z	Qatar (State of)
A8A-A8Z	Liberia (Republic of)
A9A-A9Z	Bahrain (State of)
BAA-BZZ	China (People's Republic of)
CAA-CEZ	Chile
CFA-CKZ	Canada
CLA-CMZ	Cuba
CNA-CNZ	Morocco (Kingdom of)
COA-COZ	Cuba
CPA-CPZ	Bolivia (Republic of)
CQA-CUZ	Portugal
CVA-CXZ	Uruguay (Eastern Republic of)
CYA-CZZ	Canada
C2A-C2Z	Nauru (Republic of)
C3A-C3Z	Andorra (Principality of)
C4A-C4Z	Cyprus (Republic of)
C5A-C5Z	Gambia (Republic of the)
C6A-C6Z	Bahamas (Commonwealth of the)
C7A-C7Z	World Meteorological Organization
C8A-C9Z	Mozambique (Republic of)
DAA-DRZ	Germany (Federal Republic of)
DSA-DTZ	Korea (Republic of)
DUA-DZZ	Philippines (Republic of the)
D2A-D3Z	Angola (Republic of)
D4A-D4Z	Cape Verde (Republic of)
D5A-D5Z	Liberia (Republic of)
D6A-D6Z	Comoros (Islamic Federal Republic of the)
D7A-D9Z	Korea (Republic of)
EAA-EHZ	Spain
EIA-EJZ	Ireland
EKA-EKZ	Armenia (Republic of)
ELA-ELZ	Liberia (Republic of)
EMA-EOZ	Ukraine
EPA-EQZ	Iran (Islamic Republic of)
ERA-ERZ	Moldova (Republic of)
ESA-ESZ	Estonia (Republic of)
ETA-ETZ	Ethiopia (Federal Democratic Republic of)
EUA-EWZ	Belarus (Republic of)
EXA-EXZ	Kyrgyz Republic
EYA-EYZ	Tajikistan (Republic of)
EZA-EZZ	Turkmenistan
E2A-E2Z	Thailand
E3A-E3Z	Eritrea
E4A-E4Z	Palestinian Authority

E5A-E5Z	New Zealand - Cook Islands (WRC-07)
E7A-E7Z	Bosnia and Herzegovina (Republic of) (WRC-07)
FAA-FZZ	France
GAA-GZZ	United Kingdom of Great Britain and Northern Ireland
HAA-HAZ	Hungary (Republic of)
HBA-HBZ	Switzerland (Confederation of)
HCA-HDZ	Ecuador
HEA-HEZ	Switzerland (Confederation of)
HFA-HFZ	Poland (Republic of)
HGA-HGZ	Hungary (Republic of)
HHA-HHZ	Haiti (Republic of)
HIA-HIZ	Dominican Republic
HJA-HKZ	Colombia (Republic of)
HLA-HLZ	Korea (Republic of)
HMA-HMZ	Democratic People's Republic of Korea
HNA-HNZ	Iraq (Republic of)
HOA-HPZ	Panama (Republic of)
HQA-HRZ	Honduras (Republic of)
HSA-HSZ	Thailand
HTA-HTZ	Nicaragua
HUA-HUZ	El Salvador (Republic of)
HVA-HVZ	Vatican City State
HWA-HYZ	France
HZA-HZZ	Saudi Arabia (Kingdom of)
H2A-H2Z	Cyprus (Republic of)
H3A-H3Z	Panama (Republic of)
H4A-H4Z	Solomon Islands
H6A-H7Z	Nicaragua
H8A-H9Z	Panama (Republic of)
IAA-IZZ	Italy
JAA-JSZ	Japan
JTA-JVZ	Mongolia
JWA-JXZ	Norway
JYA-JYZ	Jordan (Hashemite Kingdom of)
JZA-JZZ	Indonesia (Republic of)
J2A-J2Z	Djibouti (Republic of)
J3A-J3Z	Grenada
J4A-J4Z	Greece
J5A-J5Z	Guinea-Bissau (Republic of)
J6A-J6Z	Saint Lucia
J7A-J7Z	Dominica (Commonwealth of)
J8A-J8Z	Saint Vincent and the Grenadines
KAA-KZZ	**United States of America**
LAA-LNZ	Norway
LOA-LWZ	Argentine Republic

LXA-LXZ	Luxembourg
LYA-LYZ	Lithuania (Republic of)
LZA-LZZ	Bulgaria (Republic of)
L2A-L9Z	Argentine Republic
MAA-MZZ	United Kingdom of Great Britain and Northern Ireland
NAA-NZZ	**United States of America**
OAA-OCZ	Peru
ODA-ODZ	Lebanon
OEA-OEZ	Austria
OFA-OJZ	Finland
OKA-OLZ	Czech Republic
OMA-OMZ	Slovak Republic
ONA-OTZ	Belgium
OUA-OZZ	Denmark
PAA-PIZ	Netherlands (Kingdom of the)
PJA-PJZ	Netherlands (Kingdom of the) - Netherlands Antilles
PKA-POZ	Indonesia (Republic of)
PPA-PYZ	Brazil (Federative Republic of)
PZA-PZZ	Suriname (Republic of)
P2A-P2Z	Papua New Guinea
P3A-P3Z	Cyprus (Republic of)
P4A-P4Z	Netherlands (Kingdom of the) - Aruba
P5A-P9Z	Democratic People's Republic of Korea
RAA-RZZ	Russian Federation
SAA-SMZ	Sweden
SNA-SRZ	Poland (Republic of)
SSA-SSM	Egypt (Arab Republic of)
SSN-STZ	Sudan (Republic of the)
SUA-SUZ	Egypt (Arab Republic of)
SVA-SZZ	Greece
S2A-S3Z	Bangladesh (People's Republic of)
S5A-S5Z	Slovenia (Republic of)
S6A-S6Z	Singapore (Republic of)
S7A-S7Z	Seychelles (Republic of)
S8A-S8Z	South Africa (Republic of)
S9A-S9Z	Sao Tome and Principe (Democratic Republic of)
TAA-TCZ	Turkey
TDA-TDZ	Guatemala (Republic of)
TEA-TEZ	Costa Rica
TFA-TFZ	Iceland
TGA-TGZ	Guatemala (Republic of)
THA-THZ	France
TIA-TIZ	Costa Rica
TJA-TJZ	Cameroon (Republic of)
TKA-TKZ	France

TLA-TLZ	Central African Republic
TMA-TMZ	France
TNA-TNZ	Congo (Republic of the)
TOA-TQZ	France
TRA-TRZ	Gabonese Republic
TSA-TSZ	Tunisia
TTA-TTZ	Chad (Republic of)
TUA-TUZ	Côte d'Ivoire (Republic of)
TVA-TXZ	France
TYA-TYZ	Benin (Republic of)
TZA-TZZ	Mali (Republic of)
T2A-T2Z	Tuvalu
T3A-T3Z	Kiribati (Republic of)
T4A-T4Z	Cuba
T5A-T5Z	Somali Democratic Republic
T6A-T6Z	Afghanistan (Islamic State of)
T7A-T7Z	San Marino (Republic of)
T8A-T8Z	Palau (Republic of)
UAA-UIZ	Russian Federation
UJA-UMZ	Uzbekistan (Republic of)
UNA-UQZ	Kazakhstan (Republic of)
URA-UZZ	Ukraine
VAA-VGZ	Canada
VHA-VNZ	Australia
VOA-VOZ	Canada
VPA-VQZ	United Kingdom of Great Britain and Northern Ireland
VRA-VRZ	China (People's Republic of) - Hong Kong
VSA-VSZ	United Kingdom of Great Britain and Northern Ireland
VTA-VWZ	India (Republic of)
VXA-VYZ	Canada
VZA-VZZ	Australia
V2A-V2Z	Antigua and Barbuda
V3A-V3Z	Belize
V4A-V4Z	Saint Kitts and Nevis
V5A-V5Z	Namibia (Republic of)
V6A-V6Z	Micronesia (Federated States of)
V7A-V7Z	Marshall Islands (Republic of the)
V8A-V8Z	Brunei Darussalam
WAA-WZZ	**United States of America**
XAA-XIZ	Mexico
XJA-XOZ	Canada
XPA-XPZ	Denmark
XQA-XRZ	Chile
XSA-XSZ	China (People's Republic of)
XTA-XTZ	Burkina Faso

XUA-XUZ	Cambodia (Kingdom of)
XVA-XVZ	Viet Nam (Socialist Republic of)
XWA-XWZ	Lao People's Democratic Republic
XXA-XXZ	China (People's Republic of) - Macao (WRC-07)
XYA-XZZ	Myanmar (Union of)
YAA-YAZ	Afghanistan (Islamic State of)
YBA-YHZ	Indonesia (Republic of)
YIA-YIZ	Iraq (Republic of)
YJA-YJZ	Vanuatu (Republic of)
YKA-YKZ	Syrian Arab Republic
YLA-YLZ	Latvia (Republic of)
YMA-YMZ	Turkey
YNA-YNZ	Nicaragua
YOA-YRZ	Romania
YSA-YSZ	El Salvador (Republic of)
YTA-YUZ	Serbia (Republic of) (WRC-07)
YVA-YYZ	Venezuela (Republic of)
Y2A-Y9Z	Germany (Federal Republic of)
ZAA-ZAZ	Albania (Republic of)
ZBA-ZJZ	United Kingdom of Great Britain and Northern Ireland
ZKA-ZMZ	New Zealand
ZNA-ZOZ	United Kingdom of Great Britain and Northern Ireland
ZPA-ZPZ	Paraguay (Republic of)
ZQA-ZQZ	United Kingdom of Great Britain and Northern Ireland
ZRA-ZUZ	South Africa (Republic of)
ZVA-ZZZ	Brazil (Federative Republic of)
Z2A-Z2Z	Zimbabwe (Republic of)
Z3A-Z3Z	The Former Yugoslav Republic of Macedonia
2AA-2ZZ	United Kingdom of Great Britain and Northern Ireland
3AA-3AZ	Monaco (Principality of)
3BA-3BZ	Mauritius (Republic of)
3CA-3CZ	Equatorial Guinea (Republic of)
3DA-3DM	Swaziland (Kingdom of)
3DN-3DZ	Fiji (Republic of)
3EA-3FZ	Panama (Republic of)
3GA-3GZ	Chile
3HA-3UZ	China (People's Republic of)
3VA-3VZ	Tunisia
3WA-3WZ	Viet Nam (Socialist Republic of)
3XA-3XZ	Guinea (Republic of)
3YA-3YZ	Norway
3ZA-3ZZ	Poland (Republic of)
4AA-4CZ	Mexico
4DA-4IZ	Philippines (Republic of the)
4JA-4KZ	Azerbaijani Republic

4LA-4LZ	Georgia (Republic of)
4MA-4MZ	Venezuela (Republic of)
4OA-4OZ	Montenegro (Republic of) (WRC-07)
4PA-4SZ	Sri Lanka (Democratic Socialist Republic of)
4TA-4TZ	Peru
4UA-4UZ	United Nations
4VA-4VZ	Haiti (Republic of)
4WA-4WZ	Democratic Republic of Timor-Leste (WRC-03)
4XA-4XZ	Israel (State of)
4YA-4YZ	International Civil Aviation Organization
4ZA-4ZZ	Israel (State of)
5AA-5AZ	Libya (Socialist People's Libyan Arab Jamahiriya)
5BA-5BZ	Cyprus (Republic of)
5CA-5GZ	Morocco (Kingdom of)
5HA-5IZ	Tanzania (United Republic of)
5JA-5KZ	Colombia (Republic of)
5LA-5MZ	Liberia (Republic of)
5NA-5OZ	Nigeria (Federal Republic of)
5PA-5QZ	Denmark
5RA-5SZ	Madagascar (Republic of)
5TA-5TZ	Mauritania (Islamic Republic of)
5UA-5UZ	Niger (Republic of the)
5VA-5VZ	Togolese Republic
5WA-5WZ	Samoa (Independent State of)
5XA-5XZ	Uganda (Republic of)
5YA-5ZZ	Kenya (Republic of)
6AA-6BZ	Egypt (Arab Republic of)
6CA-6CZ	Syrian Arab Republic
6DA-6JZ	Mexico
6KA-6NZ	Korea (Republic of)
6OA-6OZ	Somali Democratic Republic
6PA-6SZ	Pakistan (Islamic Republic of)
6TA-6UZ	Sudan (Republic of the)
6VA-6WZ	Senegal (Republic of)
6XA-6XZ	Madagascar (Republic of)
6YA-6YZ	Jamaica
6ZA-6ZZ	Liberia (Republic of)
7AA-7IZ	Indonesia (Republic of)
7JA-7NZ	Japan
7OA-7OZ	Yemen (Republic of)
7PA-7PZ	Lesotho (Kingdom of)
7QA-7QZ	Malawi
7RA-7RZ	Algeria (People's Democratic Republic of)
7SA-7SZ	Sweden
7TA-7YZ	Algeria (People's Democratic Republic of)

7ZA-7ZZ	Saudi Arabia (Kingdom of)
8AA-8IZ	Indonesia (Republic of)
8JA-8NZ	Japan
8OA-8OZ	Botswana (Republic of)
8PA-8PZ	Barbados
8QA-8QZ	Maldives (Republic of)
8RA-8RZ	Guyana
8SA-8SZ	Sweden
8TA-8YZ	India (Republic of)
8ZA-8ZZ	Saudi Arabia (Kingdom of)
9AA-9AZ	Croatia (Republic of)
9BA-9DZ	Iran (Islamic Republic of)
9EA-9FZ	Ethiopia (Federal Democratic Republic of)
9GA-9GZ	Ghana
9HA-9HZ	Malta
9IA-9JZ	Zambia (Republic of)
9KA-9KZ	Kuwait (State of)
9LA-9LZ	Sierra Leone
9MA-9MZ	Malaysia
9NA-9NZ	Nepal
9OA-9TZ	Democratic Republic of the Congo
9UA-9UZ	Burundi (Republic of)
9VA-9VZ	Singapore (Republic of)
9WA-9WZ	Malaysia
9XA-9XZ	Rwandese Republic
9YA-9ZZ	Trinidad and Tobago

Third-Party Communications and Amateur Radio

If all of this information about ham radios is somewhat intimidating, do not despair. "You" can still use ham radios for communications without being a licensed operator. Yes, you do have to have a ham license in order to legally transmit by ham equipment (or be under the direct supervision of someone else who is licensed), but there is an alternative – third-party communication.

Third-party communications occur when a licensed operator sends either written or verbal messages on behalf of unlicensed persons or organizations. There are two "controls" on third-party communication.

First, the communication must be noncommercial and of a personal nature. Asking a ham operator to contact another ham operator located in an area just hit by tornados and, because of being without power, phones do not work in Grandma Sally's city so you can check up on her, is okay. Asking a ham to send a message out that you have an old Chevy for sale would not be okay.

Second, the message must be going to a permitted area. Transmitting from a US location to another US location is okay, but transmitting from the US to another country may not. Because third-party communications bypass a country's normal telephone and postal systems, many foreign governments forbid such communications. In order to transmit from one country to another, the other country must have signed a third-party agreement with the US. What follows is a list of those countries that do have third-party a communications agreement with the US.

V2	Antigua / Barbuda
LU	Argentina
VK	Australia
V3	Belize
CP	Bolivia
T9	Bosnia-Herzegovina
PY	Brazil
VE	Canada
CE	Chile
HK	Colombia
D6	Comoros (Federal Islamic Republic of)
TI	Costa Rica
CO	Cuba
HI	Dominican Republic
J7	Dominica
HC	Ecuador
YS	El Salvador
C5	Gambia, The
9G	Ghana
J3	Grenada
TG	Guatemala
8R	Guyana
HH	Haiti
HR	Honduras
4X	Israel
6Y	Jamaica
JY	Jordan
EL	Liberia
V7	Marshall Islands
XE	Mexico
V6	Micronesia, Federated States of
YN	Nicaragua
HP	Panama
ZP	Paraguay
OA	Peru
DU	Philippines
VR6	Pitcairn Island

V4	St. Christopher / Nevis
J6	St. Lucia
J8	St. Vincent and the Grenadines
9L	Sierra Leone
ZS	South Africa
3DA	Swaziland
9Y	Trinidad / Tobago
TA	Turkey
GB	United Kingdom
CX	Uruguay
YV	Venezuela
4U1ITUITU	Geneva
4U1VICVIC	Vienna

Remember, before TSHTF, keep your pantry well stocked, your powder dry, and your batteries fully charged. 73

APPENDIX A

American Radio Relay League

Affiliated Amateur Radio Clubs in

Wyoming

ARRL Affiliated Club	**Big Horn Basin Amateur Radio Club**
City:	Basin, WY
Call Sign:	KI7W
Section:	WY
ARRL Affiliated Club	**Platte River Amateur Radio Community Association**
City:	Casper, WY
Call Sign:	KE7JMU
Section:	WY
ARRL Affiliated Club	**Casper Amateur Radio Club**
City:	Casper, WY
Call Sign:	W7VNJ
Section:	WY
Links:	casperarc.net
ARRL Affiliated Club	**SHY-WY Amateur Radio Club**
City:	Cheyenne, WY
Call Sign:	KC7SNO
Section:	WY
Links:	http://www.shywyarc.net
ARRL Affiliated Club	**Northeast Wyoming Amateur Radio Association**
City:	Gillette, WY
Call Sign:	NE7WY
Section:	WY
Links:	www.newara.vcn.com
ARRL Affiliated Club	**Sweetwater County Amateur Radio**
City:	Green River, WY
Call Sign:	WY7U
Section:	WY
Links:	www.wy7u.org
ARRL Affiliated Club	**Jackson Hole Area Amateur Radio Club**
City:	Jackson, WY
Call Sign:	K7JAC
Section:	WY
Links:	www.jhaarc.org
ARRL Affiliated Club	**University Amateur Radio Club**
City:	Laramie, WY
Call Sign:	N7UW
Section:	WY
Links:	www.uwyo.edu/uarc

ARRL Affiliated Club   **Cloud Peak Radio & Electronics Group**
City: Sheridan, WY
Call Sign: WY7SHR
Section: WY
Links: cloudpeak.wetpaint.com

ARRL Affiliated Club   **Great Plains Amateur Repeater Association**
City: Wheatland, WY
Call Sign: WA7SNU
Section: WY

APPENDIX B

Amateur Radio License Holders

in

Wyoming
(by City)

Call Sign: KF6TRI
Lisa Draney
1926 Dry Creek Rd
Afton WY 83110

Call Sign: KA1GSX
Robert A Wells
215 E 9th Ave
Afton WY 83110

Call Sign: N7DHZ
David M Jolley
85 Easy Acres Loop
Afton WY 83110

Call Sign: N7FWT
Wanda L Jolley
85 Easy Acres Loop
Afton WY 83110

Call Sign: KD7NTY
Larry G Fluckiger
3611 Hiway 241
Afton WY 83110

Call Sign: KD7NMQ
Kristine Anderson
61 Hwy 241
Afton WY 83110

Call Sign: KE7JD
Geoffory D Anderson
1190 Hwy 241
Afton WY 83110

Call Sign: N7CRV
Geoffory D Anderson
1190 Hwy 241
Afton WY 83110

Call Sign: K7LRA

Lincoln County Races
Support Group
1865 Hwy 241
Afton WY 83110

Call Sign: KE7OYS
Lincoln County Races
Support Group
1865 Hwy 241
Afton WY 83110

Call Sign: K7LEV
Leveda L Troy
1865 Hwy 241
Afton WY 83110

Call Sign: KE7QLE
Leveda L Troy
1865 Hwy 241
Afton WY 83110

Call Sign: N9ABM
Charles M Jones
3964 Hwy 241
Afton WY 831101656

Call Sign: KD7ZEZ
Loren M Norman
209 Madison Ave
Afton WY 83110

Call Sign: N7VXV
Jim D Allred
Rt 1
Afton WY 83110

Call Sign: KB7YMP
Reese E Jeppsen
512 St Hwy 236
Afton WY 83110

Call Sign: K3CTR
Eugene F Troy
1865 State Hwy 241
Afton WY 831109766

Call Sign: KD7IJD
Wesley D Cranney
329 W Papworth Ln
Afton WY 83110

Call Sign: KB7RLC
Annette J Cassity
Afton WY 83110

Call Sign: KD7RUX
Kenneth A Belveal
Afton WY 83110

Call Sign: N7VGS
Barton C Cassity
Afton WY 83110

Call Sign: KD7PHN
Devin J Cassity
Afton WY 83110

Call Sign: KD7QIW
Laura J Finch
Afton WY 83110

Call Sign: KD7PHO
Rory D Finch
Afton WY 83110

Call Sign: KC7MHE
George W Hare Jr
Afton WY 83110

Call Sign: KC7WRH
Charles T Hare
Afton WY 83110

Call Sign: KD7HMT
John K Haws
Afton WY 83110

Call Sign: KD7LKQ
Anna D Helm
Afton WY 831101479

Call Sign: WB7OQG
Thomas P Matthews
Afton WY 83110

Call Sign: KA7ECQ
David B Sears
Afton WY 831100708

Call Sign: KE7MWR
Brian E Walton
Afton WY 83110

Call Sign: KD7ZEY
Diane Spencer
Afton WY 83110

Call Sign: KE7QIS
Franchot L Olson
Afton WY 83110

Call Sign: KF7SKZ
John W Holtgreve
Afton WY 83110

Call Sign: KD7YHW
Linda L Hare
Afton WY 83110

FCC Amateur Radio Licenses in Aladdin

Call Sign: KF0LE
Duane A Chafee
56 Hay Creek Rd
Aladdin WY 82710

Call Sign: WA8WLO
Donald L Hughes
3996 Rt 24
Aladdin WY 82710

FCC Amateur Radio Licenses in Albin

Call Sign: KE7RQB
Darro J Nekuda
300 Walcott St
Albin WY 82050

Call Sign: KB7VQU
Phillip R Brooks
Albin WY 82050

FCC Amateur Radio Licenses in Alpine

Call Sign: W8DSV
Robert C Christie
694 Alpine Hills Dr
Alpine WY 83128

Call Sign: AE4NO
Bruce C Schweitzer
278 Pine St
Alpine WY 83128

Call Sign: WB6VTH
Thomas G Coletti
62 Ruth Rd
Alpine WY 83128

Call Sign: KD7OHL
James R Bean
Alpine WY 83128

Call Sign: KB7VUO
Tami J Bean
Alpine WY 83128

Call Sign: KA7DRB
Lee M Hinkel
Alpine WY 83128

Call Sign: N7BMI
William R Oliver
Alpine WY 83128

Call Sign: KA7LDR
Don L Peterson

Alpine WY 831283106

Call Sign: KD7DBK
Calvin B Williams
Alpine WY 83128

Call Sign: KB1OAB
Dennis K Clancy
Alpine WY 83128

Call Sign: KE7IRN
Eric A Baker
Alpine WY 83128

Call Sign: WY7A
Eric A Baker
Alpine WY 83128

Call Sign: WY7USA
Eric A Baker
Alpine WY 83128

Call Sign: W7JHW
James R Bean
Alpine WY 83128

FCC Amateur Radio Licenses in Avta

Call Sign: KA7YLW
Douglas A Dirks
228 River Rd
Alva WY 82711

Call Sign: KF7MOW
Roger T Shea
75 Table Rock E Rd
Alva WY 83414

FCC Amateur Radio Licenses in Atlantic City

Call Sign: AB7UQ
Thomas C Weber
100 Atlantic City Rd

Atlantic City WY 82520

FCC Amateur Radio Licenses in Auburn

Call Sign: KC7OPU
Ivan K Bruderer
531 Toms Canyon Rd
Auburn WY 83111

Call Sign: AD7CM
Rick Linford
33 Wagon Rut Ln
Auburn WY 83111

Call Sign: N7SIA
Kevin S Lewis
30 Worton Ln
Auburn WY 83111

FCC Amateur Radio Licenses in Baggs

Call Sign: KS0COP
Mark M Lapinskas
Baggs WY 82321

Call Sign: KD7UZJ
Wesley R Kudera
Baggs WY 82321

FCC Amateur Radio Licenses in Banner

Call Sign: K6MKX
Dana R Schlicting
1096 Hwy 14E
Banner WY 82832

Call Sign: W7MKX
Dana R Schlicting
1096 Hwy 14E
Banner WY 82832

Call Sign: W7DOT

Dorothy J Schlicting
1096 Hwy 14E
Banner WY 82832

Call Sign: KF7UYO
Bryan K King
24 Soux Rd
Banner WY 82832

Call Sign: KG6FAT
Philip B Smith
5 W Sioux Rd
Banner WY 82832

Call Sign: KD7ZSQ
Philip B Smith
5 W Sioux Rd
Banner WY 82832

FCC Amateur Radio Licenses in Bar Nunn

Call Sign: KD7BBS
Michael W Mc Daniel Sr
4950 Antelope Dr
Bar Nunn WY 82601

Call Sign: KH6JVF
William J Woods
5210 Belvista
Bar Nunn WY 82601

Call Sign: WA6SYK
Alfred J Dynarski Jr
1101 Prairie Ln
Bar Nunn WY 82601

Call Sign: W7SYK
Alfred J Dynarski Jr
1101 Prairie Ln
Bar Nunn WY 82601

Call Sign: KI7YY
Nyland K Pearson
2854 Sunset Blvd

Bar Nunn WY 82601

FCC Amateur Radio Licenses in Basin

Call Sign: N7NQA
David L Sanders
4049 Golf Course Rd
Basin WY 82410

Call Sign: KB7BWD
Edward C Brayton
4054 Golf Course Rd
Basin WY 82410

Call Sign: N7YGM
Jeanne A Mumm
505 Montana Ave
Basin WY 82410

Call Sign: N7YGN
Jeff P Mumm
505 Montana Ave
Basin WY 82410

Call Sign: KF7DPL
Ashley N Davis
4960 Orchard Bench Rd
Basin WY 82410

Call Sign: KF7DPM
Julie M Davis
4960 Orchard Bench Rd
Basin WY 82410

Call Sign: WD4BLM
Johnny K Davis Mr.
4960 Orchard Bench Rd
Basin WY 82410

Call Sign: WB7S
Jerry L Pyle
905 S 9th
Basin WY 82410

Call Sign: WB7SUE
Susan M Pyle
905 S 9th
Basin WY 82410

Call Sign: KZ7V
Harry Holloway Jr
Basin WY 82410

Call Sign: K7LEO
Leo A Miller
Basin WY 82410

Call Sign: KC7TJT
Stephen E Crane
Basin WY 82410

Call Sign: KD7BXB
Penny L Miller
Basin WY 82410

Call Sign: KD7AHC
Garth A Reid Jr
Basin WY 82410

Call Sign: KD7BKT
James A Schave
Basin WY 82410

Call Sign: KE7MTD
Andrew Smith
Basin WY 82410

Call Sign: KE7MTE
Rainey D Smith
Basin WY 82410

FCC Amateur Radio Licenses in Bedford

Call Sign: KD7BHE
Joseph K Nicholes
200 A St
Bedford WY 83112

Call Sign: KE7OZD
O'Dell Merritt
4421 Co Rd 123
Bedford WY 83112

Call Sign: W7UY
Robert P Giese
501 Lone Star Rd
Bedford WY 831120277

Call Sign: KD7LVE
Star Valley Amateur Radio
Club
501 Lone Star Rd
Bedford WY 831120277

Call Sign: N5DXD
Jennifer M Giese
501 Lone Star Rd Box
4277
Bedford WY 831120277

Call Sign: N5KXN
Robert P Giese
501 Lone Star Rd Box
4277
Bedford WY 831120277

Call Sign: KD7GEA
Brad R Nelson
140 Willowcreek Canyon
Rd
Bedford WY 83112

Call Sign: WZ7B
Brad R Nelson
140 Willowcreek Canyon
Rd
Bedford WY 83112

Call Sign: KC5CZ
Michael F Burton
Bedford WY 83112

Call Sign: KD7GQX

Dan C Jenkins
Bedford WY 83112

Call Sign: W5PB
Shelby Amateur Radio
Club
Bedford WY 831120277

Call Sign: KD7GEB
Jermy B Wight
Bedford WY 83112

Call Sign: KE7TYC
Morris A Stewart
Bedford WY 83112

Call Sign: KF7FFY
Randy L Plowman
Bedford WY 83112

FCC Amateur Radio Licenses in Beulah

Call Sign: N7TBD
Paul N Smith
807 Rifle Pit Rd
Beulah WY 827128804

Call Sign: N7YBW
Violet R Smith
807 Rifle Pit Rd
Beulah WY 827128804

FCC Amateur Radio Licenses in Big Horn

Call Sign: K7JTR
Jeanne T Roelfsema
4 W Fork
Big Horn WY 82833

Call Sign: WB7UTK
Millard D Rhodes
Big Horn WY 82833

Call Sign: KN7S
Neil Savin
Big Horn WY 82833

Call Sign: W7SVN
Neil Savin
Big Horn WY 82833

FCC Amateur Radio Licenses in Big Piney

Call Sign: N7XCU
Curtis L Hendricks
24 1st North Rd
Big Piney WY 83113

Call Sign: N7OYL
Laura M Hendricks
24 1st North Rd
Big Piney WY 83113

Call Sign: N7TLQ
Bryan P Hendricks
17 Meadow Canyon Dr
Big Piney WY 831131257

Call Sign: KC7BJY
Jon A Colson
Big Piney WY 83113

Call Sign: KD7NZW
Nicole S Colson
Big Piney WY 83113

Call Sign: W7ILL
Monte Norris
Big Piney WY 831130427

Call Sign: KF7TDF
Daniel M Wilson
Big Piney WY 83113

Call Sign: KD7WCO
Eric S Peterson
Big Piney WY 83113

Call Sign: KA7EAT
Gordon M Petty II
Big Piney WY 83113

Call Sign: KE7HPR
Gordon M Petty II
Big Piney WY 83113

Call Sign: KC7NIK
Nicole S Colson
Big Piney WY 83113

FCC Amateur Radio Licenses in Bill

Call Sign: KI0IN
William C Thompson
50 Nellie St
Bill WY 826339710

FCC Amateur Radio Licenses in Boulder

Call Sign: WB2RJR
Martin P Granica
PO Box 247
Boulder WY 82923

Call Sign: W7YP
Dave Pavel
Boulder WY 82923

Call Sign: W0OWB
James R Mc Lellan
Boulder WY 82923

FCC Amateur Radio Licenses in Buffalo

Call Sign: KA7NRG
Joseph G Kalus IV
608 Circle Dr
Buffalo WY 82834

Call Sign: KF7UYR
Connor R Oaks
120 Dally Ln
Buffalo WY 82834

Call Sign: KF7OBB
William C Ross
8935 Hwy 16 W Apt 80
Buffalo WY 82834

Call Sign: KF7UYQ
Brian T Desch
6 Jade Ct
Buffalo WY 82834

Call Sign: W7TZZ
James M Shirey
988 N Burritt Ave
Buffalo WY 82834

Call Sign: KF7PHM
Shonna L Shirey
988 N Burritt Ave
Buffalo WY 82834

Call Sign: KA7NRH
Richard S Madsen
1020 N Carrington
Buffalo WY 82834

Call Sign: NL7UI
Gerald W Eastwood
596 N Main St
Buffalo WY 82834

Call Sign: K5ABQ
Robert M Atwood
503 N Pinnacle Dr
Buffalo WY 82834

Call Sign: W7BWY
Robert M Atwood
503 N Pinnacle Dr
Buffalo WY 82834

Call Sign: W8ATX
Dave L Costello
23 Trabing Ln
Buffalo WY 82834

Call Sign: N8LXI
Patricia A Costello
23 Trabing Ln
Buffalo WY 82834

Call Sign: KE7BKV
Tom A Pearce
377 US Hwy 16 E
Buffalo WY 82834

Call Sign: W7AOC
Tom A Pearce
377 US Hwy 16 E
Buffalo WY 82834

Call Sign: K3EX
Daryl J George
395 US Hwy 16 E
Buffalo WY 828349514

Call Sign: N3HCG
Ruthann George
395 US Hwy 16 E
Buffalo WY 828349522

Call Sign: KF7PHL
Susan J Pearce
377 US Hwy 16E
Buffalo WY 82834

Call Sign: KE7QVQ
Anthony E Kyriss
300 W Fetterman 207
Buffalo WY 82834

Call Sign: WB0PST
Shirley M Wilson
450 W Lott St
Buffalo WY 828341644

Call Sign: KF7PHP
Janice C Harnish
450 Walters St
Buffalo WY 82834

Call Sign: KD7ATT
Harry T Latham
Buffalo WY 82834

Call Sign: W7QQA
Leonard D Pearce
Buffalo WY 82834

Call Sign: W7PND
Raymond L Pearce
Buffalo WY 82834

Call Sign: KF7LYZ
Anthony A Adams
Buffalo WY 82834

**FCC Amateur Radio
Licenses in Buford**

Call Sign: N7RVO
Richard F Stephen
Buford WY 82052

**FCC Amateur Radio
Licenses in Burlington**

Call Sign: AA7MU
Lowell E Card
Burlington WY 824110095

Call Sign: N7YGQ
Linnie Neves
Burlington WY 82411

Call Sign: N7YGP
Lyle J Neves
Burlington WY 82411

**FCC Amateur Radio
Licenses in Burns**

Call Sign: NC7O
Ralph E Bartels
304 Abilene Loop
Burns WY 82053

Call Sign: WB7GR
Gregory L Rix
3939 Antelope Meadows
Dr
Burns WY 82053

Call Sign: KC7NGM
Linda S Rix
3939 Antelope Meadows
Dr
Burns WY 82053

Call Sign: KJ7HN
Gerald R Birge
4570 Canvas Back Ln
Burns WY 82053

Call Sign: N7ISS
Robert L Taylor
1368 Harding Rd
Burns WY 820539605

Call Sign: KB7VZZ
James E Abel Jr
114 Luther Ave
Burns WY 82053

Call Sign: KE7YUL
Jeffrey E Brown
1155 Rd 148
Burns WY 82053

Call Sign: KF7CJD
Gary A Lyon
4906 Rd 218
Burns WY 82053

Call Sign: N7QJA
Douglas W Elgin

1109 W Miltrose Dr
Burns WY 82053

Call Sign: KD7LVJ
Raymond A Aitken
Burns WY 82053

Call Sign: KE7YUJ
Chad A Smith
Burns WY 82053

FCC Amateur Radio Licenses in Byron

Call Sign: K6SUB
Robert V Grater
Byron WY 824120249

Call Sign: K7KLE
Sandy J Mc Gee
Byron WY 82412

Call Sign: KF7KLE
Sandy J Mc Gee
Byron WY 82412

Call Sign: K6SUB
Sandy J Mc Gee
Byron WY 82412

FCC Amateur Radio Licenses in Carpenter

Call Sign: KE7YUK
Kirby J Murdoch
4668 Cord 208
Carpenter WY 82054

Call Sign: KB3BYK
James L Newswanger Jr
582 CR 143
Carpenter WY 820549101

Call Sign: KD7VW
James E Abel Jr

745 CR 144
Carpenter WY 82054

Call Sign: KI7KC
Cleveland Harper
253 CR 148
Carpenter WY 82054

Call Sign: KA6VRW
Richard H Brant
4073 CR 209
Carpenter WY 82054

Call Sign: KB7PVC
Joe J Poelma
4829 Rd 201
Carpenter WY 82054

Call Sign: KD7ILH
Bridge Creek Radio Club
4655 Rd 207
Carpenter WY 82054

Call Sign: NT7A
Bridge Creek Radio Club
4655 Rd 207
Carpenter WY 82054

Call Sign: KO7X
Alan A Brubaker
881 West Rd
Carpenter WY 82054

Call Sign: K7MZY
Eileen E Brubaker
881 West Rd
Carpenter WY 82054

FCC Amateur Radio Licenses in Casper

Call Sign: N7RRA
Clarence E Darling Sr
5034 Alcovart Box 22
Casper WY 82604

Call Sign: N7BZZ
Steve E Welch
3060 Allendale Blvd
Casper WY 82601

Call Sign: KC7JBF
Billy L Bachler
4780 Antelope Dr
Casper WY 82601

Call Sign: AE7LU
Billy L Bachler
4780 Antelope Dr
Casper WY 82601

Call Sign: KB7TFB
Greg D Avey
4361 Arroyo
Casper WY 82604

Call Sign: WA7ZAC
James B Sayler
3248 Aspen Dr
Casper WY 82601

Call Sign: KB7WJS
Steven M Jenkins
3305 Aspen Dr
Casper WY 82601

Call Sign: KJ7ZR
Reginald D Atkins
6687 Bailey Pl
Casper WY 82604

Call Sign: W7HYW
Herbert J Haass
1123 Beaumont
Casper WY 82601

Call Sign: KF7BLU
Randy A Mcdonald
2136 Begonia St
Casper WY 82604

Call Sign: W7BLM
Robert L Meyer
2504 Bellaire Dr
Casper WY 826043158

Call Sign: W7TOY
Susan R Meyer
2504 Bellaire Dr
Casper WY 826043158

Call Sign: KA7HCO
Harold K Hansen
2604 Bellaire Dr
Casper WY 82604

Call Sign: N7JNO
Art G Hurlbut Jr
2501 Belmont
Casper WY 82604

Call Sign: KC7WFP
Roger D Larson
1414 Birch
Casper WY 82604

Call Sign: KJ7KK
Melvin B Smith
2450 Bonnie Brae St
Casper WY 826015801

Call Sign: KB7YP
James F Doyle
1219 Bretton
Casper WY 82601

Call Sign: KC7WYG
Fort Caspar Repeater
Association
1219 Bretton Dr
Casper WY 826093145

Call Sign: WW7WY
Fort Caspar Repeater
Association

1219 Bretton Dr
Casper WY 826093145

Call Sign: KE7OQ
Milton E Carshon
1420 Brookview Dr
Casper WY 82601

Call Sign: KE7ZCP
Carolyn J Boyd
6326 Buckboard Rd Unit 1
Casper WY 82604

Call Sign: WA9ZDT
Lawrence A Heintzman
3400 Carmel Dr
Casper WY 82604

Call Sign: KB0GQZ
Charles H Decker
1675 Chamber Lain Rd
Casper WY 82604

Call Sign: K7SLM
Earl Hilterbrand
1420 Chamberlain Rd
Casper WY 82604

Call Sign: KF7OPS
Sean A Huber
3075 Cold Springs Rd
Casper WY 82604

Call Sign: KC7CNL
Charles L Norris
281 Columbine
Casper WY 82604

Call Sign: N7COD
Daniel M York
1520 Cornwall
Casper WY 82609

Call Sign: N7COE
Lohriene G York

1520 Cornwall
Casper WY 82609

Call Sign: KD7AGA
Cdk Net
1730 Cornwall St
Casper WY 82609

Call Sign: KC7NGN
Michael R Sullivan
1534 Crimson Dawn Rd
Casper WY 82601

Call Sign: KF7CFY
Bruce Mcdonald
50 Dahlia St
Casper WY 82604

Call Sign: KC7TOR
Bernice E Mason
605 E 11th St
Casper WY 82601

Call Sign: N7YMD
David J Mertz
2501 E 12th
Casper WY 82609

Call Sign: KB7CCK
Ray F Patterson
4018 E 12th St
Casper WY 82609

Call Sign: N7RQQ
Dennis M Murrell
3841 E 15th 422
Casper WY 82609

Call Sign: W7TIF
Tiffany R Lancaster
3841 E 15th St 104
Casper WY 82609

Call Sign: KB7DTX
Jacques P Herter

2510 E 15th St 3
Casper WY 82609

3531 E 22nd
Casper WY 82609

2668 E 7th
Casper WY 82609

Call Sign: KB7ECO
Kathleen E Herter
2510 E 15th St 3
Casper WY 82609

Call Sign: N7YMB
Neil E Coupens
3632 E 23rd
Casper WY 82609

Call Sign: KE7EYX
Lee A Simon
3870 E 8th St Apt 205
Casper WY 82609

Call Sign: N7IX
Michael G Petera
5130 E 16th St
Casper WY 82609

Call Sign: W5JPW
James P Wilhite
3521 E 24th St
Casper WY 82609

Call Sign: NG7T
Mark A Knittle
4090 E Magnolia
Casper WY 82604

Call Sign: N7WSC
Charles W Hale
643 E 17th St
Casper WY 82601

Call Sign: K7TAQ
Robert O Sannerud
1931 E 2nd St
Casper WY 82601

Call Sign: KE7JMU
Platte River Amateur
Radio Community
Association
4090 E Magnolia
Casper WY 82604

Call Sign: AC7IU
Frank D Martin
812 E 18th
Casper WY 82601

Call Sign: WA4ZLT
Robert T Davis Jr
3014 E 2nd St
Casper WY 82609

Call Sign: KD7ABE
Michael A Jaramillo
842 E Yellowstone 13
Casper WY 82601

Call Sign: N7YMC
Jess M Spencer
5130 E 18th St
Casper WY 82609

Call Sign: KE6FKD
Kendall C Ebert
829 E 4th St Apt 1
Casper WY 82601

Call Sign: AE7EB
Mark K Warner
12355 Engburg
Casper WY 82604

Call Sign: KC5PY
Nikolai Kerpchar
4441 E 18th St
Casper WY 82609

Call Sign: WB7EWT
David B Mac Carter
3022 E 5th
Casper WY 82601

Call Sign: AK7MW
Mark K Warner
12355 Engburg
Casper WY 82604

Call Sign: KF7GNB
Charles L Snyder
3840 E 18th St Apt 806
Casper WY 82609

Call Sign: AA7AY
Robert E Jones
2245 E 5th St
Casper WY 82609

Call Sign: KC7ZKB
Raymond Feeney
2101 Esses
Casper WY 82604

Call Sign: N7RQY
Craig W Warner
1225 E 22nd
Casper WY 82601

Call Sign: W7LCF
James A Mc Coy
2734 E 6th St
Casper WY 82609

Call Sign: KC7UGE
Clifford A Gindulis
1411 Falcon Crest Blvd
Casper WY 82601

Call Sign: K7QGV
William A Rader II

Call Sign: N7SEA
Betty A Krause

Call Sign: KE7AZH
Heather Belden
2116 Fontenelle
Casper WY 82604

Call Sign: N0IPL
Wilton J Barnum
2905 Garden Creek Rd
Casper WY 82601

Call Sign: N7PBO
Robert C Adams
3240 Green Meadows Dr
Casper WY 82604

Call Sign: KE7AZG
Stephen L Belden
2116 Fontenelle
Casper WY 82604

Call Sign: KC7CTW
Randall D Evans
4802 Glen Dr
Casper WY 82604

Call Sign: W7DPB
Douglas P Barone
4110 Grizzly
Casper WY 82604

Call Sign: KC7ZRU
Tate E Belden
2116 Fontenelle St
Casper WY 826043748

Call Sign: KC7LQG
William C Doll
1961 Glendale
Casper WY 82601

Call Sign: WA7NXX
Marvin R Wockovich
3104 Hamilton Way
Casper WY 82601

Call Sign: KA7O
Tate E Belden
2116 Fontenelle St
Casper WY 826043748

Call Sign: KA6YLH
Jason W Whaley
2021 Glendale Ave
Casper WY 826014940

Call Sign: KE7LNW
Theodore E Fisher
3650 Harvey Pl 119
Casper WY 82601

Call Sign: KM7S
Francis T Pfeiffer
943 Foster Rd
Casper WY 82601

Call Sign: N7NDZ
Mark T Westby
2335 Glendale Ave
Casper WY 82601

Call Sign: KC6PLL
Kenneth A Siedenburg
3073 Herrington Dr
Casper WY 82604

Call Sign: N7SDY
Jim K Fritz
1812 Fremont
Casper WY 82604

Call Sign: KF7TJI
Michael W Magee
2018 Glendo
Casper WY 82604

Call Sign: KC6OUZ
Charles R Siedenburg
3073 Herrington Dr
Casper WY 82604

Call Sign: KB7UNL
Linda L Boyer
2004 Fremont Ave
Casper WY 82604

Call Sign: KE7DWB
Amy M Sherwin
631 Goodstein
Casper WY 82601

Call Sign: KF7KNL
James W Coberly
8940 Hopi
Casper WY 82601

Call Sign: N7VLM
Stacy J Boyer
2004 Fremont Ave
Casper WY 82604

Call Sign: KE7DWC
Michelle E Sherwin
631 Goodstein
Casper WY 82601

Call Sign: KE5OUO
Dennis C Bienvenu
399 Indian Paintbrush
Casper WY 82604

Call Sign: N7RQW
Charles L Osterloh
2919 Garden Cir Rd
Casper WY 82601

Call Sign: N7TGO
John P Sherwin
631 Goodstein Dr
Casper WY 82601

Call Sign: N7PIN
Dennis C Bienvenu
399 Indian Paintbrush
Casper WY 82604

Call Sign: KI4TJI
Jim E Dobbins
3351 Indian Scout Dr
Casper WY 82604

Call Sign: N7NPC
Jay L Martin
1441 Ivy Ln
Casper WY 82609

Call Sign: KB7FYN
Lynn M Martin
1441 Ivy Ln
Casper WY 82609

Call Sign: W7DRJ
Jay L Martin
1441 Ivy Ln
Casper WY 82609

Call Sign: KD7NUC
Carol S Layton
1824 Jim Bridger
Casper WY 82604

Call Sign: AB7GW
Jack M Murphy
1220 Kelly Dr
Casper WY 82609

Call Sign: KC7EFY
Joan D Murphy
1220 Kelly Dr
Casper WY 82609

Call Sign: W0RVP
Elmer H Peters
1563 Kelly Dr
Casper WY 826093653

Call Sign: KE7ZCS
Jared D Kelly
6621 King Salmon
Casper WY 82604

Call Sign: KK5RI
Diane D Mc Kee
2035 Kingsbury
Casper WY 82609

Call Sign: KQ5R
James C Mc Kee
2035 Kingsbury
Casper WY 82609

Call Sign: KA7EGZ
Curtis C Breikjern
1240 Kingston
Casper WY 82601

Call Sign: WA7MIO
Alvin E Olson
2630 Knollwood Dr
Casper WY 82604

Call Sign: KC7NVJ
David J Muir
760 Landmark Dr
Casper WY 82609

Call Sign: KB7SKE
Jennifer L Hubenthal
1908 Lilac
Casper WY 82604

Call Sign: KD7LJH
Bryce L Garner
2024 Linda Vista
Casper WY 82609

Call Sign: KC7WTI
Nathan Mm Stratton
1227 Locust
Casper WY 82604

Call Sign: N7DBI
Robert R Miller
496 Long Ln
Casper WY 826092402

Call Sign: KD7LLK
Alan K Hill
2621 Lynn Ln
Casper WY 82601

Call Sign: K7GLL
Elmer S Parson Jr
83 Magnolia
Casper WY 82604

Call Sign: KC7MJI
Christine E Knittle
4090 Magnolia
Casper WY 82604

Call Sign: KE7UJC
Trevor J Evans
1400 Manor Dr
Casper WY 82609

Call Sign: KB7UNK
Michael T Harrington II
1421 Manor Dr
Casper WY 82609

Call Sign: KB7UHP
Mary L Harrington
1421 Manor Dr
Casper WY 82609

Call Sign: KD7ITX
Darrell W Sanders
85 Marigold
Casper WY 82604

Call Sign: W7MZW
Morres P Morgensen
125 Marigold
Casper WY 82601

Call Sign: WA7RMI
Karen A Brannon
2220 Mariposa Blvd
Casper WY 82604

Call Sign: N7UOI
Michael L Overeem
3520 Medicine Bow
Casper WY 82609

Call Sign: KD7BBQ
Bill D Conway Jr
725 N Beech
Casper WY 82601

Call Sign: WA7YGC
Robert A Brown
333 N Mc Kinley
Casper WY 826012209

Call Sign: N6EOV
Frances L Martin
2015 Miracle Dr
Casper WY 826094601

Call Sign: KC7NAM
Bill D Conway
725 N Beech
Casper WY 82601

Call Sign: KB7SKH
Glenn E Anderson
334 N Nebraska
Casper WY 82609

Call Sign: AG6V
Robert G Martin
2015 Miracle Dr
Casper WY 826094601

Call Sign: KF7KNJ
Floyd B Bennett
1250 N Center St 111
Casper WY 82601

Call Sign: KJ7EO
Dale C Hubenthal
144 N Pennsylvania Ave
Casper WY 82609

Call Sign: KE6EUI
Brian C Lindgren
1912 Miracle Dr
Casper WY 82609

Call Sign: N7EUE
Russell G Humphreys
232 N Colorado
Casper WY 82609

Call Sign: N7ALI
Donnie J Claunch
3441 Navarre Rd
Casper WY 82604

Call Sign: W6NJ
Brian C Lindgren
1912 Miracle Dr
Casper WY 82609

Call Sign: K7KMT
Steven L Fritz
166 N Elk St
Casper WY 82601

Call Sign: KC5WVZ
Ralph D Johnson
2092 Nottingham Dr
Casper WY 82609

Call Sign: KB7TSU
Debbie S Whitaker
3425 Monte Vista
Casper WY 82601

Call Sign: KA7AHP
Robert M Robinson
351 N Forest Dr
Casper WY 82609

Call Sign: KB0NMR
Jennifer Flowers
8935 Osage Rd
Casper WY 826017449

Call Sign: KI7MG
Rohm P Whitaker
3425 Monte Vista
Casper WY 82601

Call Sign: KC0RJG
Timothy J Flores
901 N Kimball St
Casper WY 82601

Call Sign: KB0NJL
Larry E Flowers
8935 Osage Rd
Casper WY 826017449

Call Sign: KB0MIQ
Jacen E Avery
688 N 3rd Ave
Casper WY 82604

Call Sign: W7XF
James D Howard
124 N Lennox
Casper WY 82601

Call Sign: N6VUQ
Thomas A Suffel
2710 Osprey St
Casper WY 82601

Call Sign: WB7NWN
William L Crimm
96 N 4th Ave
Casper WY 82604

Call Sign: K7WRS
Minnie R Brown
333 N Mc Kinley
Casper WY 82601

Call Sign: KC7WFO
Harold F Buhler Jr
3020 Pheasant Dr
Casper WY 826044304

Call Sign: NK7H
Daniel B Rea
2906 Pheasant Dr
Casper WY 82604

Call Sign: AE7EC
Michael W Hopkins
3043 Robertson Rd
Casper WY 82604

Call Sign: KE7ESD
Andrew K Temme
3301 S Coffman
Casper WY 82604

Call Sign: WA7LUY
Carlton L Hunter
644 Pineview Pl
Casper WY 82609

Call Sign: N7IUS
Cork W Conde
1429 S Bonnie Brae
Casper WY 82601

Call Sign: KB7UHQ
Michael E Mammon
3600 S Coffman
Casper WY 82604

Call Sign: N7SAE
Cynthia J Poe
3890 Plateau
Casper WY 82604

Call Sign: KC7JBG
Donald W Link
1926 S Cedar
Casper WY 82601

Call Sign: KB7UHR
Starla C Mammon
3600 S Coffman
Casper WY 82604

Call Sign: N7UOJ
Paul L Goedicke
413 Pleasant St
Casper WY 826019009

Call Sign: W7SXV
John J Mc Cue
1325 S Center St
Casper WY 82601

Call Sign: N7SEF
Kimberley E Mammon
3120 S Coffman Ave
Casper WY 82604

Call Sign: N7MIN
Donald E Oakes
6753 Poison Spider Rd
Casper WY 82604

Call Sign: WB7CBH
Roger E La France
5021 S Center St
Casper WY 82604

Call Sign: N7RRB
Shawn M Mammon
3120 S Coffman Ave
Casper WY 82604

Call Sign: N7ZRP
Sam J Cordova IV
4472 Pursel Dr
Casper WY 82604

Call Sign: KD0WA
Roger C Kline
5111 S Center St
Casper WY 82601

Call Sign: N7XKR
Stewart K Anderson
1777 S Conwell St
Casper WY 82601

Call Sign: N7PRY
Jason Vanderlinden
3515 Quail Ln
Casper WY 82604

Call Sign: WA7EMO
Richard G Kingsolver
1607 S Chestnut
Casper WY 82601

Call Sign: WA6ZGV
Curtis L Stroh
842 S Durbin
Casper WY 82601

Call Sign: KA7JUN
Joshua H Cruse
4122 Ranch Rd
Casper WY 82604

Call Sign: KB7WOJ
Connie L Doll
5499 S Coates Rd
Casper WY 82604

Call Sign: NU7S
Ardeth A Lobet
1105 S Durbin St
Casper WY 82601

Call Sign: KE7ZCO
Joshua H Cruse
4122 Ranch Rd
Casper WY 82604

Call Sign: AC7DW
William C Doll
5499 S Coates Rd
Casper WY 82604

Call Sign: W7HE
Robert M Mc Keown
1105 S Durbin St
Casper WY 826014327

Call Sign: N7SDX
Carol J Hurlbut
1614 S Fairdale
Casper WY 82601

Call Sign: WB7RDQ
Craig M Post
2202 S Fairdale
Casper WY 82601

Call Sign: KC7CTX
Laura J Brown
104 S Fenway
Casper WY 82601

Call Sign: W7TVK
James S Anderson
1120 S Forest Dr
Casper WY 82609

Call Sign: KE7ICZ
Mark T Adams
314.5 S Grant
Casper WY 82601

Call Sign: KD7OJJ
David M Rippley
902 S Grant Ave
Casper WY 82604

Call Sign: KF7QYF
Larry E Ash
1527 S Jackson
Casper WY 82601

Call Sign: K7SEN
Robert D Long
324 S Kimball
Casper WY 82602

Call Sign: N7RQV
Thomas M Miller
2004 S Lennox St
Casper WY 82601

Call Sign: KB7RPU
Don C Kuenz
1425 S Lowell
Casper WY 82601

Call Sign: KC7SWM
Stephen G Wilson
2630 S Mc Kinley B
Casper WY 82601

Call Sign: K7DKZ
Lawrence G Fritz
517 S Mc Kinley St
Casper WY 82601

Call Sign: WA7GOV
Brian R Propp
609 S Mc Kinley St
Casper WY 82601

Call Sign: WB6WCO
Ted R Jacobs
845 S Mckinley St
Casper WY 82601

Call Sign: KE7NPF
Warren R Appel
1900 S Missouri 2426
Casper WY 82609

Call Sign: KE7ZCT
Tiffany R Appel
1900 S Missouri Apt 2426
Casper WY 82609

Call Sign: K7RXC
Paul R Long
1900 S Missouri St Apt
3333
Casper WY 826093342

Call Sign: KC7UOQ
Edward C Boyer
1339 S Mitchell
Casper WY 82601

Call Sign: W7CQL
Wayne M Moore
142 S Montana
Casper WY 82601

Call Sign: N7TDJ
Peter V Dewees
1124 S Nebraska Ave
Casper WY 82609

Call Sign: KC7ITH
Lesa K Wright
914 S Oak St
Casper WY 82601

Call Sign: KE6CNU
Matthew L Hickok
5610 S Oak St
Casper WY 826016428

Call Sign: W7BHH
Joseph H Prochaska
1615 S Pine St
Casper WY 82604

Call Sign: KD7YBM
Sean R Collister
1435 S Pine St
Casper WY 82604

Call Sign: N7SUP
Neva W Cole
S Poplar 91
Casper WY 82601

Call Sign: K4AMA
Vernon W Hutchinson
3600 S Poplar St
Casper WY 82601

Call Sign: K9DR
Daniel A Roberts
3723 S Poplar St
Casper WY 826015959

Call Sign: WA6ONW
Lyle S Bray
S Poplar St 75
Casper WY 826016103

Call Sign: N7SDZ
Arthur G Hurlbut Sr
2108 S Richard
Casper WY 82601

Call Sign: WA7DLK
Richard M Roberts
1504 S Spruce
Casper WY 826014156

Call Sign: KB7NL
Donald H Little
119 S Utah
Casper WY 82609

Call Sign: N7ZRQ
James H Cooper
1610 S Walnut
Casper WY 82601

Call Sign: WA7YZQ
Steven C Kirkwood
6220 S Walnut
Casper WY 82601

Call Sign: KC7YRA
Bradley B Lutz
2001 S Washington
Casper WY 82601

Call Sign: KE7ZCR
Jennifer L Lutz
2001 S Washington St
Casper WY 82601

Call Sign: KC7YQY
David C Gowers
1755 S Wilson
Casper WY 82601

Call Sign: N7RPS
Edward A Schebler Jr
1415 S Wolcott
Casper WY 82601

Call Sign: N0KTM
Kenneth L Nuss
53 Sagebrush
Casper WY 82604

Call Sign: N7SDV
Albert Mc Connell
7800 Salt Creek 37
Casper WY 82601

Call Sign: KE7UJE
Thomas G Rorabaugh
7297 Sharrock Rd
Casper WY 82604

Call Sign: KC7WDJ
Corey J Laymon
2212 Shattuck Ave
Casper WY 82601

Call Sign: KC7FHU
Charles H Larsen
1507 Sheridan Dr
Casper WY 82604

Call Sign: KK7WG
Charles H Larsen
1507 Sheridan Dr
Casper WY 82604

Call Sign: KC7HOI
Imogene Z Larsen
1507 Sheridan Dr
Casper WY 82604

Call Sign: WA7NHP
Leo A Bush
1143 So Durbin
Casper WY 82601

Call Sign: W7YWE
Frederick L Hildebrand
4015 Somerset Cir
Casper WY 82609

Call Sign: KA7QJQ
Keith L Ames
4033 Somerset Cir
Casper WY 82609

Call Sign: N7RQX
Donald W Mc Hattie
824 St Mary
Casper WY 82601

Call Sign: KE7DHF
John A Mchattie
824 St Mary
Casper WY 82601

Call Sign: N7OSW
Barry C Poe
5009 Stoneridge Way
Casper WY 82601

Call Sign: W7IEC
Donald J Jacobson
4431 Sunrise Dr
Casper WY 826045107

Call Sign: KE7AZF
Mike K Coley
1001 Sussex
Casper WY 82609

Call Sign: K7SAN
Sandi L Bachmeier
607 Swanton
Casper WY 82609

Call Sign: AB7BJ
Timothy E Bachmeier
607 Swanton Ave
Casper WY 82609

Call Sign: KE7GIA
Stephen J Murphy
3520 Teton
Casper WY 82609

Call Sign: KE7HBQ
Lance L Lyon
1301 Trojan Dr
Casper WY 82609

Call Sign: KD7JLN
Jean Fowkes
1755 W 27
Casper WY 82604

Call Sign: WY7TED
Theodore E Fisher
510 Thelma Dr
Casper WY 82609

Call Sign: N7XWK
Kathy L Morton
1341 Trojan Dr
Casper WY 82609

Call Sign: KD7MHS
Jean Fowkes
1755 W 27
Casper WY 82604

Call Sign: KA4DJY
George L Curtis Jr
301 Thelma Dr 149
Casper WY 82609

Call Sign: WS7W
Warren G Morton
1341 Trojan Dr
Casper WY 82609

Call Sign: N7RQR
Kent L Macklin
2601 W 39th
Casper WY 82604

Call Sign: KE7DDR
George L Curtis Jr
301 Thelma Dr 149
Casper WY 82609

Call Sign: W7AYH
Charles R Thrapp
20255 US Hwy W 20-26
Casper WY 826049597

Call Sign: KE6UDE
Michael S Amick
2101 W 39th St
Casper WY 82604

Call Sign: N6HRZ
Cecil J Henry
301 Thelma Dr 401
Casper WY 82609

Call Sign: WC7Y
David A Ericson
94 Valley Dr
Casper WY 82604

Call Sign: WA5DGI
Michael A Megee
4341 W 40th St
Casper WY 826044438

Call Sign: KF6DVR
Daniel B Gorath
301 Thelma Dr 145
Casper WY 82609

Call Sign: KB7AIX
Adam L Heady
231 W 10th
Casper WY 82601

Call Sign: N7DGI
Michael A Megee
4341 W 40th St
Casper WY 826044438

Call Sign: KF7VBW
Ebenezer K Howe IV
301 Thelma Dr 441
Casper WY 82609

Call Sign: KD7EFQ
Matthew Todd Miskel
804.5 W 13th St
Casper WY 82601

Call Sign: KE7VS
Clifford N Bloomenrader
Jr
2049 W 43rd
Casper WY 82604

Call Sign: KL7DE
Michael S Downing
301 Thelma Dr Apt 209
Casper WY 82609

Call Sign: WA7IFJ
Kelly E Hudson
1033 W 23rd St
Casper WY 82604

Call Sign: WD0AVD
Robert L Schulz
2100 W 44th St
Casper WY 82604

Call Sign: KA7DYX
Ronald H Sizemore
1665 Trojan
Casper WY 82609

Call Sign: N7PXK
Edward R Mueller
1113 W 25th St
Casper WY 82604

Call Sign: KA7VNE
Randall U Kinnamon
721 W 45th St

Casper WY 82601

Casper WY 82601

Casper WY 82604

Call Sign: KA7RCO
Douglas P Barone
3720 W 45th St
Casper WY 82604

Call Sign: KC7ZBZ
Karen Harrison
1754 W Coffman
Casper WY 82604

Call Sign: KD7EFS
Christopher S Arthur
1640 Westridge Way
Casper WY 82604

Call Sign: KC7PCU
Eric K Hansen
721 W 50th St
Casper WY 82605

Call Sign: N7SEG
James W Harrison
1754 W Coffman Ave
Casper WY 82604

Call Sign: KF0E
Joseph E Finney
1704 Westridge Way
Casper WY 82604

Call Sign: KF0HC
Jeffrey L Elliott
640 W 53rd St
Casper WY 82601

Call Sign: KC6PLK
Michele M Siedenburg
131 W G St
Casper WY 82601

Call Sign: WY7W
Stephen J Murphy
4970 Yesness Ct
Casper WY 82604

Call Sign: KC7JFT
Peter S White
721 W 55th St
Casper WY 82601

Call Sign: KC7CTZ
Martha M Robinson
3801 W Ormsby Rd
Casper WY 826017433

Call Sign: W7TSM
Dennis E Nicholson
1320 Yorkshire Ave
Casper WY 82609

Call Sign: N5ZAF
Lonnie A Teague
770 W 58th St
Casper WY 82601

Call Sign: KA7CFU
John F Goedicke
6385 W Ter Alcova Rt
Casper WY 82604

Call Sign: N3YEN
Edward J Mc Kenna
37 Yucca Circle
Casper WY 826045303

Call Sign: N5XYD
Michelle K Teague
770 W 58th St
Casper WY 82601

Call Sign: KA7CFV
Judith A Goedicke
6385 W Terrace Alcova Rt
Casper WY 82604

Call Sign: KB7UHO
Ben A Hubenthal
Casper WY 82605

Call Sign: KI7MH
Robert S Wedlock
Casper WY 82609

Call Sign: KA6COH
Edwin J Blase
1030 W 60th St
Casper WY 826016252

Call Sign: N7ZRN
Michael A Cutright
6015 W Zero Rd
Casper WY 82604

Call Sign: N7LUB
Oscar J Whitlock
Casper WY 82609

Call Sign: WA7COH
Edwin J Blase
1030 W 60th St
Casper WY 826016252

Call Sign: N7XKS
Greg R Hansen
1170 Waterford
Casper WY 82609

Call Sign: W7PAW
Lewis L Baker
Casper WY 82602

Call Sign: KF7LFN
Benlee A Pentecost
222 W B St Apt 114B

Call Sign: N0AXE
David A Allerheiligen
4935 Webb Creek Rd

Call Sign: N7SVW
Dennis R Booth

Casper WY 82602

Call Sign: W7VNJ
Casper Amateur Radio
Club
Casper WY 82601

Call Sign: WB7SNA
Curtis V Fletcher
Casper WY 826050564

Call Sign: N7HVM
William B Gibbins
Casper WY 82602

Call Sign: KC5ECP
Patrick D Herman
Casper WY 82602

Call Sign: W7PSO
James A Masterson
Casper WY 82602

Call Sign: N7CKQ
John A Masterson
Casper WY 82602

Call Sign: KD7VHZ
Diane G Tyler
Casper WY 82602

Call Sign: K1JXN
John M Jackson
Casper WY 826052273

Call Sign: KF7VBU
Kenneth T Brown
Casper WY 82605

Call Sign: KF7BLV
Louard Crumbaugh IV
Casper WY 82602

Call Sign: K0AT
Fredrick B Benson
Centennial WY 820550178

Call Sign: WS7C
Robert M Hansen
Centennial WY 82055

Call Sign: KD7ZNX
Logan L Grant
1113 Adams Ave
Cheyenne WY 82001

Call Sign: KA7FZM
Clarence W R Mellott
1303 Adams Ave
Cheyenne WY 82001

Call Sign: N4RTW
John T Shaffer
1505 Adams Ave
Cheyenne WY 820016407

Call Sign: KC7RZL
Karyn L Williams
3318 Alexander Ave
Cheyenne WY 82001

Call Sign: KA7SBE
Lawrence V Velte
1802 Andover Dr
Cheyenne WY 82001

Call Sign: KE7HGN
Robert R Sanson
1836 Andover Dr
Cheyenne WY 82001

Call Sign: KB1DEC
Sheri L Feeley
314 Arbor Ln

Cheyenne WY 82009

Call Sign: KE7HWO
Robert F Osban
7618 Archies Rd
Cheyenne WY 82001

Call Sign: WA7GYQ
Thomas E Armstrong
9549 Aspen Pointe Ln
Cheyenne WY 82009

Call Sign: K7VTN
Lowell E Thomas
3813 Atkin Ct
Cheyenne WY 82001

Call Sign: KD7KXC
Burdette J Reed
5035 Atlantic Dr
Cheyenne WY 820019675

Call Sign: KD7ZNW
Wyoming Wing - Civil Air
Patrol
5116 Atlantic Dr
Cheyenne WY 82001

Call Sign: WY4CAP
Wyoming Wing - Civil Air
Patrol
5116 Atlantic Dr
Cheyenne WY 82001

Call Sign: N7RQZ
William A Collister
5116 Atlantic Dr
Cheyenne WY 820016902

Call Sign: KE7SZZ
Aaron A Wesson
Atlas Loop
Cheyenne WY 82001

Call Sign: KB7LHZ

Thomas R Thibeault
Atlas Loop
Cheyenne WY 82001

Call Sign: KF7RBP
Ryan L Robinson
3408 Baldwin Dr
Cheyenne WY 82001

Call Sign: N7NMY
Robert H Ray
3914 Baldwin Dr
Cheyenne WY 82001

Call Sign: W7QP
Warren O Rumsey
10514 Beartooth Dr
Cheyenne WY 82009

Call Sign: KF7CJL
William E Hutchinson
264 Bent Ave
Cheyenne WY 82007

Call Sign: KB7USI
Brooke W Hefner
2803 Bent Ave
Cheyenne WY 82001

Call Sign: KB7WCL
Robert C Mathews III
3503 Bevans St
Cheyenne WY 82001

Call Sign: AA7QV
Robert C Mathews Jr
3503 Bevans St
Cheyenne WY 82001

Call Sign: K7FDL
Robert C Mathews Jr
3503 Bevans St
Cheyenne WY 82001

Call Sign: WC7AAF

Wyoming Emergency
Management Agency
5500 Bishop Blvd
Cheyenne WY 82009

Call Sign: KF7QFH
Randy W Miller
1310 Blossom Ct
Cheyenne WY 82007

Call Sign: KC7OYD
Eric L Millhouse
3133 Bluff Pl
Cheyenne WY 82009

Call Sign: KB0NNG
Troy M Brandt
3153 Bluff Place
Cheyenne WY 82009

Call Sign: KE7SZS
Brian M Chapman
6834 Bomar Dr
Cheyenne WY 82009

Call Sign: N7JPR
Frederic D Dumire
7212 Bomar Dr
Cheyenne WY 82009

Call Sign: KG7K
Frederic D Dumire
7212 Bomar Dr
Cheyenne WY 82009

Call Sign: WA7RRV
Georg Jensen
705 Bonanza Trl
Cheyenne WY 82009

Call Sign: N7HTS
Gary D Krause
7003 Bonneville Pl
Cheyenne WY 82009

Call Sign: W7IFD
James H Hess
3623 Bradley
Cheyenne WY 82001

Call Sign: N1KDL
Beth F Gianetti
1905 Bradley Avenue
Cheyenne WY 82001

Call Sign: N1FEB
Gilbert P Gianetti
1905 Bradley Avenue
Cheyenne WY 82001

Call Sign: WA7EGK
Robert R Rule
5318 Braehill Rd
Cheyenne WY 82009

Call Sign: KF7KEZ
Rayann Brown
7809 Braehill Rd
Cheyenne WY 82009

Call Sign: KC7ZLY
Michael C Mccabe
8914 Braehill Rd
Cheyenne WY 82009

Call Sign: K7ZDX
Larry G Porter
1007 Briar Ct
Cheyenne WY 82007

Call Sign: KF7QHD
Carl C Bosselman
10510 Buck Brush Rd
Cheyenne WY 82009

Call Sign: KC7WOV
Danny J Poelma
8351 Buckboard Rd
Cheyenne WY 82009

Call Sign: KF7UNG
Kyle D Hoffdahl
4728 Cactus Way
Cheyenne WY 82009

Call Sign: WA5AEY
Leonard L Nash
1834 Cadillac Rd
Cheyenne WY 82009

Call Sign: W7EIN
Gregg G Wood
901 Cahill Dr
Cheyenne WY 82001

Call Sign: KD7LLL
Howard F Heiduck
1004 Cahill Dr
Cheyenne WY 82001

Call Sign: KF9MG
Jeremy D Spranger
805 Cahill Dr
Cheyenne WY 82001

Call Sign: N7WMQ
Betty A Schrader
3615 Campstool Rd
Cheyenne WY 820071802

Call Sign: N7NKD
Robert W Schrader
3615 Campstool Rd
Cheyenne WY 820071802

Call Sign: WC7AAP
Laramie County
Emergency Management
Agcy
2020 Capitol Ave
Cheyenne WY 82001

Call Sign: N7IGC
Joseph E Feldman
3001 Capitol Ave

Cheyenne WY 82001

Call Sign: KC7EZF
Wade Brorby
2120 Capitol Ave Ste 2018
Cheyenne WY 82001

Call Sign: N7YNL
Rupert E Farr
2710 Carey Ave
Cheyenne WY 82001

Call Sign: KD7CSA
Kelly D Burt
4102 Carla Dr
Cheyenne WY 82009

Call Sign: KC7ISQ
Edwin J Carlson
4409 Carmel
Cheyenne WY 82009

Call Sign: KG6FHB
Clinton W Wright
1185 Carpenter Place
Cheyenne WY 82009

Call Sign: W7IFW
John L Aurzada
431 Carriage Dr
Cheyenne WY 820092088

Call Sign: NX2R
Salvatore J Palumbo
1000 Centennial Dr
Cheyenne WY 82001

Call Sign: N7MJ
Jackie L Mitchell
1141 Centennial Dr
Cheyenne WY 82001

Call Sign: KD4KPX
Robert H Lett
3904 Central Ave 107

Cheyenne WY 82001

Call Sign: KC7KHF
Cedar S Chapman
1811 Cheyenne Pl
Cheyenne WY 82001

Call Sign: KC7YJE
John D Hall
322 Chris Loop
Cheyenne WY 82007

Call Sign: KE7OML
Kimberly S Hall
322 Chris Loop
Cheyenne WY 82007

Call Sign: KD0GPA
Elaine M Frankhouser
9143 Clear Sky Dr
Cheyenne WY 82009

Call Sign: K7MXG
Jeffrey E Frankhouser
9143 Clear Sky Dr
Cheyenne WY 82009

Call Sign: KA7CWO
Jean M Harris
840 Cleveland Ave
Cheyenne WY 82001

Call Sign: KD7OXU
William V Walters
1518 Cleveland Ave
Cheyenne WY 82001

Call Sign: KD7PFE
Robin A Walters
1518 Clevelend Ave
Cheyenne WY 820016400

Call Sign: K7STN
Virgil L White
3112 Cochise Rd

Cheyenne WY 82009

Call Sign: AC7NK
Karl F Newkirk
3577 Cody Ln
Cheyenne WY 82009

Call Sign: KD7JUY
Karl F Newkirk
3577 Cody Ln
Cheyenne WY 82009

Call Sign: WA7BYG
Richard A Selby
1216 Cole Rd
Cheyenne WY 82009

Call Sign: AB0NA
Donald G Kline
4912 Connie Dr
Cheyenne WY 820095650

Call Sign: AD7PY
Donald G Kline
4912 Connie Dr
Cheyenne WY 820095650

Call Sign: KB7GWU
Stella M Owens
4913 Continental Pl
Cheyenne WY 82001

Call Sign: KC0DGU
Ronald E Swim
5515 Continental Pl
Cheyenne WY 82001

Call Sign: AB7X
Edward C Leckman
815 Converse
Cheyenne WY 820015234

Call Sign: KD7KZO
Eric G Scott
524 Cornell Ln

Cheyenne WY 82009

Call Sign: K7JIM
James E Hassler
1160 Cottonwood Dr
Cheyenne WY 82001

Call Sign: KD7ZHU
Kristin N Hush
2317 Coulter Dr
Cheyenne WY 82009

Call Sign: KF7FYD
Christian S Borgaard
2401 Council Bluff
Cheyenne WY 82009

Call Sign: KC7DVB
Dale L Gerzetich
1466 CR 109
Cheyenne WY 82009

Call Sign: WB5PMO
Alvin Willis
2395 CR 128
Cheyenne WY 82009

Call Sign: N7IGJ
Jason W Griess
1611 CR 136
Cheyenne WY 82009

Call Sign: KC0CDQ
Todd R Ludwick
3716 CR 214
Cheyenne WY 82009

Call Sign: WA7ZXL
Darwin G Mainwaring
2531 Crazy Horse Rd
Cheyenne WY 82009

Call Sign: KB7AZI
Scott A Mainwaring
2531 Crazy Horse Rd

Cheyenne WY 82009

Call Sign: KB7NUQ
James L Edlefsen
828 Creighton St
Cheyenne WY 82009

Call Sign: KF7CIT
Adrienne Edwards
837 Creighton St
Cheyenne WY 82009

Call Sign: N7SAC
Scott A Chapman
842 Creighton St
Cheyenne WY 82009

Call Sign: N6PNR
Joseph G Ewing
939 Creighton St
Cheyenne WY 82009

Call Sign: KA7OGI
David R Miller
117 Crestline Ave
Cheyenne WY 82009

Call Sign: WA7WYW
Thomas R Lee
3411 Cribbon Ave
Cheyenne WY 82001

Call Sign: N7UIN
Richard E Erion
345 Dalcour Dr
Cheyenne WY 820093517

Call Sign: KE7AZI
Thomas P Mahon
5241 Danielle Ct
Cheyenne WY 82009

Call Sign: WB7T
Robert A Lewis
519 Dartmouth Ln

Cheyenne WY 82009

Call Sign: N0ZNZ
Ruth A Dawson
1209 Dayshia Ln
Cheyenne WY 82007

Call Sign: N0ZNY
Janel R Jordy
1209 Dayshia Ln
Cheyenne WY 82007

Call Sign: N0KXK
John W Jordy
1209 Dayshia Ln
Cheyenne WY 82007

Call Sign: KD7PNK
William T Parker
889 Deerbrooke Trl
Cheyenne WY 82009

Call Sign: WX7CYS
Shy-Wy Skywarn Team
889 Deerbrooke Trl
Cheyenne WY 82009

Call Sign: KF7AXS
Mike A Clark
Del Range 514
Cheyenne WY 82009

Call Sign: KC0RPR
Loretta S Dynan
Dell Range Blvd 131
Cheyenne WY 82009

Call Sign: AI7F
Robert H Dynan
Dell Range Blvd 131
Cheyenne WY 82009

Call Sign: KC0PHO
Robert H Dynan
Dell Range Blvd 131

Cheyenne WY 82009

Call Sign: KF7CIY
Rich J Calton
1740 Dell Range Blvd 323
Cheyenne WY 82009

Call Sign: WA7KXW
Homer I Satchell
2738 Deming Blvd
Cheyenne WY 82001

Call Sign: KD6LHX
Bob M Machado
6621 Denise Rd
Cheyenne WY 82009

Call Sign: KD7LYV
Charles L Hall
2656 Devils Tower Rd
Cheyenne WY 82009

Call Sign: KB7HIH
Ronald R Kelso
3059 Dey Ave
Cheyenne WY 82001

Call Sign: KR7B
Kenneth E Rathbone
237 Dillon Ave
Cheyenne WY 82007

Call Sign: N7MZW
Charles D Williams
3601 Dillon Ave Apt B
Cheyenne WY 82001

Call Sign: KK7YI
Ralph E Atchley
5358 Division Ave
Cheyenne WY 820079212

Call Sign: WY7RA
Ralph E Atchley
5358 Division Ave

Cheyenne WY 820079212

Call Sign: KB7RKZ
James A Mc Keithen
2105 E 11th St
Cheyenne WY 820015226

Call Sign: KK7VA
James A Mc Keithen
2105 E 11th St
Cheyenne WY 820015226

Call Sign: N7GAU
Nels W Nelson
2705 E 11th St
Cheyenne WY 82001

Call Sign: KA7VGO
David E Rood
1620 E 12th St
Cheyenne WY 82001

Call Sign: W7UW
Hamilton W Lufkin
2416 E 12th St
Cheyenne WY 82001

Call Sign: KD7KXD
Brian A Mcnutt
4501 E 13th St
Cheyenne WY 82001

Call Sign: AD7FX
Brian A Mcnutt
4501 E 13th St
Cheyenne WY 82001

Call Sign: N7BAM
Brian A Mcnutt
4501 E 13th St
Cheyenne WY 82001

Call Sign: WB0KWY
Richard G Thoms
5714 E 13th St

Cheyenne WY 820017463   Cheyenne WY 82001   Cheyenne WY 82001

Call Sign: WB0YDA
Linda L Thoms
5714 E 13th St
Cheyenne WY 82001

Call Sign: KD7ZHV
Susan R Millheiser
406 E 17th St Apt C
Cheyenne WY 82001

Call Sign: KF7CJX
Brady J Lyles
1614 E 20th St
Cheyenne WY 82001

Call Sign: KA7BGJ
Michael J Dugas
4409 E 14th St
Cheyenne WY 82001

Call Sign: KB7DSJ
James D Sprandel
921 E 17th St Apt C6
Cheyenne WY 82001

Call Sign: N7CXR
Christine M Best
1726.5 E 21st St
Cheyenne WY 82001

Call Sign: KC7GUP
Bobby O Lunsford
5722 E 14th St
Cheyenne WY 820017465

Call Sign: KJ7FC
Beth A Wood
608 E 17th St Apt D
Cheyenne WY 82001

Call Sign: N7TMK
John D Harris
217 E 21st St
Cheyenne WY 82001

Call Sign: KF7JPU
Andrea M Palochak
2419 E 16th St
Cheyenne WY 82001

Call Sign: KC7DVA
Todd M Parkins
1417 E 18th
Cheyenne WY 82001

Call Sign: KD1PE
Robert M Kubiac
1108 E 22nd St
Cheyenne WY 82001

Call Sign: KC7MGY
Randy D Roberts
2207 E 17th St
Cheyenne WY 82001

Call Sign: KC7DDP
Susan L Parkins
1417 E 18th St
Cheyenne WY 82001

Call Sign: W7CGK
John J Hayes
1321 E 22nd St
Cheyenne WY 82001

Call Sign: KD7RQU
August B Kassin II
4513 E 17th St
Cheyenne WY 82001

Call Sign: W7SUZ
Susan L Parkins
1417 E 18th St
Cheyenne WY 82001

Call Sign: N7QIX
Bruce A Dexter
1730 E 22nd St
Cheyenne WY 82001

Call Sign: KF7DFR
Kevin E Vance
4720 E 17th St
Cheyenne WY 82001

Call Sign: W7PAR
Todd M Parkins
1417 E 18th St
Cheyenne WY 82001

Call Sign: KC7RZK
Thomas J Coles
1811 E 22nd St
Cheyenne WY 82001

Call Sign: WB7VKH
Harley F Stone
921 E 17th St Apt B8
Cheyenne WY 82001

Call Sign: AA7TB
Robert L Harrington
306 E 1st Ave
Cheyenne WY 82001

Call Sign: KD7YOF
Daniel M Ihde
1403 E 23rd St
Cheyenne WY 82001

Call Sign: KE7CWB
Jedediah J Millheiser
406 E 17th St Apt C

Call Sign: KD7LLI
Pamela S Stimson
1010 E 20th

Call Sign: W7ITC
Kenneth A Crips
1517 E 23rd St

Cheyenne WY 820014011

Cheyenne WY 82007

Cheyenne WY 82009

Call Sign: KC7KUL
Charles C Kretz
600 E 3rd St
Cheyenne WY 82007

Call Sign: KF7HMP
Adam L Ackels
717 E 7th St
Cheyenne WY 82007

Call Sign: N0IMW
Allen W Lowe
911 E Fox Farm Rd 2
Cheyenne WY 820072588

Call Sign: WB7SJB
William M Futrell Jr
305 E 4th Ave
Cheyenne WY 82001

Call Sign: N7JJY
George J Smith
1100 E 7th St
Cheyenne WY 82007

Call Sign: N0JFW
Dorothy A Lowe
911 E Fox Farm Rd 2
Cheyenne WY 820072588

Call Sign: W7SJB
William M Futrell Jr
305 E 4th Ave
Cheyenne WY 82001

Call Sign: KD7ADD
Christina M Holman
1115 E 7th St
Cheyenne WY 820079743

Call Sign: KB7MDF
Timothy E Chapman
911 E Fox Farm Rd 2
Cheyenne WY 82007

Call Sign: KB7RCZ
Keith R Bliss
305 E 4th St
Cheyenne WY 82007

Call Sign: KC7PFM
Glenn H Hein
4405 E 7th St
Cheyenne WY 82001

Call Sign: KE7YUM
Daniel L Mitchell
831 E Gopp Ct
Cheyenne WY 82007

Call Sign: K7KRB
Keith R Bliss
305 E 4th St
Cheyenne WY 82007

Call Sign: W7GHH
Glenn H Hein
4405 E 7th St
Cheyenne WY 82001

Call Sign: KC7PFN
John J Galka Jr
310 E Iowa
Cheyenne WY 82009

Call Sign: KB7FBJ
Leslie D Lorentz II
719 E 6th St
Cheyenne WY 82007

Call Sign: N7ZWB
Mary A De Hoff
4003 E 9th St
Cheyenne WY 82001

Call Sign: N7GT
Gregory T Galka
310 E Iowa
Cheyenne WY 82009

Call Sign: KD7NCO
Aimee Mobley
1203 E 6th St
Cheyenne WY 82007

Call Sign: KE7KPI
Gary W Gorny
4010 E 9th St
Cheyenne WY 82001

Call Sign: W0SHS
Scott H Stevenson Sr
304 E Jefferson Rd
Cheyenne WY 82007

Call Sign: K7OAF
Don H Piester
4215 E 6th St
Cheyenne WY 82001

Call Sign: K7HRO
Thomas E De Hoff
4003 E 9th St
Cheyenne WY 82001

Call Sign: W7JFN
James I Bruce
515 E Pershing 123
Cheyenne WY 82001

Call Sign: KD7RIM
Jack D Floyd
207 E 6th St

Call Sign: KF7CJY
Nicholas J Casner
5659 E Four Mile Rd

Call Sign: KC7OEK
Carey Junior High School
Amateur Radio Club

1780 E Pershing Blvd
Cheyenne WY 82001

Call Sign: N7FR
Robert J Fredrick
2208 E Pershing Blvd
Cheyenne WY 82001

Call Sign: KC0TFM
Gregory K Smith
7110 E Pershing Blvd
Cheyenne WY 82001

Call Sign: KG6EIC
Stephen E Jackson
4109 E Pershing Blvd Apt
L261
Cheyenne WY 82001

Call Sign: W7LYF
Edward J Rybicki
5005 E Villa Cir
Cheyenne WY 82009

Call Sign: KF6DJV
Bill M Roberts Jr
1836 Edgewater Avenue
Cheyenne WY 82009

Call Sign: W7JRF
James R Ferrall
5709 Education Dr 204
Cheyenne WY 82009

Call Sign: N7YNM
Anne M Pettrey
4303 El Camino Dr
Cheyenne WY 82001

Call Sign: KB7SRJ
Joe K Pettrey
4303 El Camino Dr
Cheyenne WY 82001

Call Sign: KC7IQH

Phillip N Crider
11807 Empire Dr
Cheyenne WY 82009

Call Sign: KA7KSJ
Catherine S Mitchell
1911 Evans Ave
Cheyenne WY 82001

Call Sign: WD4KOH
James M Moore
7521 Evers Blvd
Cheyenne WY 82009

Call Sign: KC7IJN
Errin A Davidson
4008 Everton Dr
Cheyenne WY 82009

Call Sign: KD7OCH
Richard S Dickinson Jr
301 Factor Ln
Cheyenne WY 82007

Call Sign: KF7LO
James N Bresemann Sr
3409 Fire Side Dr
Cheyenne WY 82001

Call Sign: KB7ZGN
Kay H Laub
5257 Fishing Bridge
Cheyenne WY 82009

Call Sign: KC7DUZ
Frank J Pinkley Jr
3220 Forbes Ct
Cheyenne WY 82009

Call Sign: KD6FVL
Henry E Warg
2693 Ford Rd
Cheyenne WY 82009

Call Sign: W7QPV

William D Mc Craken
3500 Forest Dr
Cheyenne WY 82001

Call Sign: WK0C
Jeffrey E Frankhouser
2 Fort Warren Ave
Cheyenne WY 82001

Call Sign: KC7WGN
Herbert F Werry
13015 Four Mile Rd
Cheyenne WY 82009

Call Sign: KC7KUN
Kelvin D Moore
3415 Foxcroft
Cheyenne WY 82001

Call Sign: KC7RHJ
Joshua L Singer
3673 Foxcroft
Cheyenne WY 82001

Call Sign: N7PLJ
George H Anderson
6509 Foxglove Dr
Cheyenne WY 820095706

Call Sign: KB7TDD
Susann C Anderson
6509 Foxglove Dr
Cheyenne WY 820095706

Call Sign: AB0E
Wayne G Bard
1622 Fremont Ave
Cheyenne WY 82001

Call Sign: KC9JAD
Robert T Smith
1844 Fremont Ave Apt 3
Cheyenne WY 82001

Call Sign: WA7HQY

Donald P Nolan
3925 Frontier Park
Cheyenne WY 82001

Donna H Goss
3458 Green Valley Rd
Cheyenne WY 82001

Earl B Whisenant
1305 Hackamore Rd
Cheyenne WY 82009

Call Sign: KE7VIA
Ralph E Doll
3524 Frontier St
Cheyenne WY 82001

Call Sign: KA0ZZK
Tracie L Peterson
5312 Greenriver Pl
Cheyenne WY 82001

Call Sign: NV0F
Lester D Scott
1920 Hackamore Rd
Cheyenne WY 82009

Call Sign: W6MXG
James B Strom
4210 Gem Trl
Cheyenne WY 82001

Call Sign: N7LAS
Robert W Le Goff
5328 Greybull Ave
Cheyenne WY 82009

Call Sign: WB7NLQ
Donald L Anders
422 Hacker Ct 1
Cheyenne WY 82009

Call Sign: KI6AJA
Teddi A Myers
2205 Gordon Rd 38
Cheyenne WY 82007

Call Sign: W7AAD
Gary R Long
5317 Greybull St
Cheyenne WY 82009

Call Sign: KE7JM
David J Hardingham
1261 Happy Jack Rd
Cheyenne WY 82009

Call Sign: N7ZAJ
Joe E Carmichael
3937 Granite St
Cheyenne WY 820011841

Call Sign: KC0QXB
Jacob F Haldi
5111 Griffith Ave
Cheyenne WY 82009

Call Sign: KF7FXW
Cole M Smith
7393 Harvest Loop
Cheyenne WY 82009

Call Sign: W7HLA
Harold M Roberts
3101 Green Valley Rd
Cheyenne WY 82001

Call Sign: KF7JPZ
Jacob F Haldi
5111 Griffith Ave
Cheyenne WY 82009

Call Sign: KB7ZWD
John M Browning
2903 Henderson
Cheyenne WY 82001

Call Sign: KA7LEM
Samuel H Romero
3174 Green Valley Rd
Cheyenne WY 82001

Call Sign: KF7CJC
Warren D Burgess
1982 Guernsey Dr
Cheyenne WY 82009

Call Sign: W7BMJ
Raymond L Routh
910 Henderson Dr
Cheyenne WY 82001

Call Sign: WA7SQJ
Wilma E Hirst
3458 Green Valley Rd
Cheyenne WY 82001

Call Sign: N7ZFQ
Warren D Burgess
1982 Guernsey Dr
Cheyenne WY 82009

Call Sign: N7TFM
John M Heller
5033 Hickory Pl
Cheyenne WY 82009

Call Sign: WA7JYO
Alan R Goss
3458 Green Valley Rd
Cheyenne WY 82001

Call Sign: KF7SAW
Thomas J Podhaski
3625 Gun Smoke Rd
Cheyenne WY 82001

Call Sign: N7SVZ
Mary Lou Burr
5102 Hickory Pl
Cheyenne WY 82009

Call Sign: WA7SOH

Call Sign: K6RST

Call Sign: AA7JQ

Roger T Burr
5102 Hickory Pl
Cheyenne WY 82009

Call Sign: KE7BVL
John D Harris
5209 Hickory Place
Cheyenne WY 82009

Call Sign: KC7CAJ
Dennis H Layman
837 Hillcrest Rd
Cheyenne WY 82001

Call Sign: KC7GUO
Sue K Layman
837 Hillcrest Rd
Cheyenne WY 82001

Call Sign: KC7GUN
Matthew G Pexton
837 Hillcrest Rd
Cheyenne WY 82001

Call Sign: N7DEN
Dennis H Layman
837 Hillcrest Rd
Cheyenne WY 82001

Call Sign: WA7JSY
Frank L Rauchfuss
4747 Hilltop Ave
Cheyenne WY 82001

Call Sign: WA7H
John S Cochrane
5409 Hilltop Ave
Cheyenne WY 82009

Call Sign: W7JSC
John S Cochrane
5409 Hilltop Ave
Cheyenne WY 82009

Call Sign: AA7IX

Martin L Mc Guffey
3116 Holland Ct
Cheyenne WY 82009

Call Sign: NH6HW
Aarne T Haas
1820 Horse Creek Rd
Cheyenne WY 820099342

Call Sign: WY7ATH
Aarne T Haas
1820 Horse Creek Rd
Cheyenne WY 820099342

Call Sign: KA0MDD
Guido Gezzi
1535 Hot Springs Apt 1
Cheyenne WY 82001

Call Sign: N7CSO
Ralph Zauner
1915 Hugur Ave
Cheyenne WY 82001

Call Sign: WD5KBH
Vernon J Anderson
4416 Huron Ave
Cheyenne WY 82001

Call Sign: KE7WQO
Susan K Stempel
3941 Hynds Blvd
Cheyenne WY 82001

Call Sign: KC7TEV
William R Morton
9601 Hynds Blvd
Cheyenne WY 82009

Call Sign: N7HHL
Robert P Smith
1067 Indiana Rd
Cheyenne WY 82003

Call Sign: AD7SY

Kevin L Gerlitz
9225 James Cole Court
Cheyenne WY 82009

Call Sign: KF7CIW
David L Dickinson
6511 Julia Rd
Cheyenne WY 82009

Call Sign: KB7LPM
Lance A Forbes
4700 King Arthur Way
Cheyenne WY 82009

Call Sign: KB0OOI
Andrew M Brewerton
911 Kingham Dr
Cheyenne WY 82001

Call Sign: KC7DVC
Michael J Sullivan
212 Lakeshore Dr
Cheyenne WY 82009

Call Sign: W7MJS
Michael J Sullivan
212 Lakeshore Dr
Cheyenne WY 82009

Call Sign: KC7UUI
Christopher S Dillingham
6117 Laramie St Unit 1
Cheyenne WY 82001

Call Sign: KF7CIU
Orion A Rice
841 Latigo Loop
Cheyenne WY 82009

Call Sign: KF7ADJ
Greg C Yarber
5620 Lawrence Ln
Cheyenne WY 82009

Call Sign: KB7CAY

Robert R Buchanan
3218 Locust Dr
Cheyenne WY 820015818

Call Sign: KC5ZSR
William W Spurrier
4705 Long Branch Loop
Cheyenne WY 82001

Call Sign: WA0MSB
Thomas H Baker
1220 Madison Ave
Cheyenne WY 82001

Call Sign: N6LKF
Gail F Sheridan
1240 Madison Avenue
Cheyenne WY 820016720

Call Sign: WB7TCG
Peggy M Woolery
7119 Manhattan Ln
Cheyenne WY 82009

Call Sign: K7TFW
Donald R Miller
7242 Manhattan Ln
Cheyenne WY 82009

Call Sign: N7JZW
Michael D More
2525 Maple Way
Cheyenne WY 82009

Call Sign: KF7CIV
Daenette More
2525 Maple Way
Cheyenne WY 82009

Call Sign: K7MKE
Michael D More
2525 Maple Way
Cheyenne WY 82009

Call Sign: KV7P

Michael D More
2525 Maple Way
Cheyenne WY 82009

Call Sign: KI7TS
Paul M Crips
7407 Maria Ln
Cheyenne WY 82009

Call Sign: W0OEI
Merton E Ward
5129 Mc Cue Dr
Cheyenne WY 82009

Call Sign: WA7KUE
Morris H Ashworth
216 Mc Farland Ave
Cheyenne WY 820072315

Call Sign: KB7QGM
Peter M Berkley
603 Mc Govern Ave
Cheyenne WY 82001

Call Sign: W7KRT
Gilbert L Crumrine
406 Mc Intyre Ln
Cheyenne WY 82007

Call Sign: KD7LLH
Daniel N Snesko
2218 Mckinney Dr
Cheyenne WY 82009

Call Sign: N3ZAW
Richard E Tashner
2231 Meadow Dr
Cheyenne WY 82001

Call Sign: KB7SWS
Donnie D Smith Jr
2024 Meadow Dr
Cheyenne WY 82001

Call Sign: N7HOF

Ronald D Williams
1835 Milton Dr
Cheyenne WY 82001

Call Sign: KA7DQH
Dale R Sullivan
6302 Moccasin
Cheyenne WY 82009

Call Sign: KD7AQJ
James L Collins
1508 Monroe Ct
Cheyenne WY 820016465

Call Sign: KD7ZGR
Beverly A Collins
1508 Monroe Ct
Cheyenne WY 82001

Call Sign: KF7FCA
Robert G Garrison
4763 Moran Ave
Cheyenne WY 82009

Call Sign: KD7KXE
David A Stokes Mr.
6551 Moreland Ave
Cheyenne WY 82009

Call Sign: W0LES
Larry E Sheridan
4718 Mountain Rd Apt
314
Cheyenne WY 820095153

Call Sign: KE7PTR
Daniel S Tolman
2336 Mugho Rd
Cheyenne WY 82009

Call Sign: KB7QOS
Martin E Jones
306 Murrary Rd
Cheyenne WY 82007

Call Sign: WB7AJG
Robert R Bachman
330 Muscadine Way
Cheyenne WY 82001

Call Sign: K7OVD
Preble L Phelps
6603 N College
Cheyenne WY 82009

Call Sign: KD7LVI
Fred W Stueve Jr
3903 N College Dr
Cheyenne WY 82001

Call Sign: WC7S
Dale E Putnam
5503 N College Dr
Cheyenne WY 820094601

Call Sign: KA7KIK
Robert L Mc Mullen
4606 N College Dr Apt
107
Cheyenne WY 820095456

Call Sign: WD8LPB
Pamela J Girt
8001 N Milliron Rd
Cheyenne WY 82009

Call Sign: KA4GTD
Brian K Miller
8001 N Milliron Rd
Cheyenne WY 82009

Call Sign: WX8O
Pamela J Girt
8001 N Milliron Rd
Cheyenne WY 82009

Call Sign: KE7HGO
Paula A Borchert
620 N Table Mt Loop
Cheyenne WY 82009

Call Sign: N7QJB
Brian D Grimm
4911 Nimmo Dr
Cheyenne WY 82009

Call Sign: KC5GNU
Terry W Higginbotham
213 Norma Ct
Cheyenne WY 82007

Call Sign: KD7KXF
Stephen H West
219 Norma Ct
Cheyenne WY 820072214

Call Sign: N7TFL
Kevin L Messman
2800 O Neil
Cheyenne WY 82001

Call Sign: N7YNK
David E Flood
2922 O Neil Ave
Cheyenne WY 82001

Call Sign: KE7BOZ
Edward D Carlson
2816 O Niel Ave
Cheyenne WY 82007

Call Sign: KF7CIZ
Kenneth W Johnson
3007 Oneil Ave
Cheyenne WY 82001

Call Sign: N7RDY
Allan M Eyres
4510 Ontario Ave
Cheyenne WY 82001

Call Sign: KD7RJN
Steven P Girt
10668 Orchard Dr
Cheyenne WY 82009

Call Sign: KF7JPY
Caleb J Johnson
1886 Packard
Cheyenne WY 82009

Call Sign: KE5NQ
James W Headstream
2377 Painted Horse Trl
Cheyenne WY 820092243

Call Sign: KI7WM
Clifford Penny
3815 Palmer St 35
Cheyenne WY 82001

Call Sign: KC7ZAB
David R White
1918 Park Ave
Cheyenne WY 820073339

Call Sign: KC7ICT
Joseph S Allen
6503 Patricia Ct
Cheyenne WY 82009

Call Sign: KE7HGM
David E Thompson
2341 Pattison Ave
Cheyenne WY 82001

Call Sign: KC7BQS
Paul J Lucas
509 Patton Ave
Cheyenne WY 82007

Call Sign: N0GOK
Jonathan R Fortune
5115 Penny Ln
Cheyenne WY 82009

Call Sign: KE0E
David A Lind
5126 Penny Ln
Cheyenne WY 82009

Call Sign: KB0YWN
Jonathan A Lind
5126 Penny Ln
Cheyenne WY 82009

Call Sign: KC7ULM
Cynthia L Collins
726 Phoenix Dr
Cheyenne WY 82001

Call Sign: KE7BCI
David N Marks
5302 Pineridge Ave
Cheyenne WY 82009

Call Sign: KE7BCH
Morgan L Marks
5302 Pineridge Ave
Cheyenne WY 82009

Call Sign: N7KFQ
William B Wright
292 Pinetree Rd
Cheyenne WY 82009

Call Sign: KI7JC
Michael B Curran
2341 Plain View
Cheyenne WY 82009

Call Sign: KB7OAA
Edward D Coelho
2408 Plainview Rd
Cheyenne WY 82009

Call Sign: K7OAA
Edward D Coelho
2408 Plainview Rd
Cheyenne WY 82009

Call Sign: K7PEC
Fredric G Hoffman Jr
2914 Plum Dr
Cheyenne WY 82001

Call Sign: KC7KUM
George C Klataske
1018 Plum St
Cheyenne WY 82003

Call Sign: KF7DFT
Paul M Draves
PO Box 20574
Cheyenne WY 82003

Call Sign: KB7PEA
James C Soden
6840 Poulos Dr
Cheyenne WY 82009

Call Sign: KC0YOS
Gregory W Ray
5510 Powderhouse Rd
Cheyenne WY 82009

Call Sign: W7LLL
Donald J Sullivan
1360 Pronghorn Ct
Cheyenne WY 82009

Call Sign: KA7UTV
Charles B Pyle
5809 Pronidence Pl
Cheyenne WY 82001

Call Sign: KE7WZE
Luis P Cantu Jr
149 Quincy Rd
Cheyenne WY 82009

Call Sign: KD7NMN
Scott A Chapman
1855 Rainbow Rd 104
Cheyenne WY 82001

Call Sign: KC7EEI
Cynthia A Macy
3425 Rawlins
Cheyenne WY 82001

Call Sign: KC0MID
Titus J Norris
2895 Rd 143
Cheyenne WY 82009

Call Sign: KD7ZHT
Michael E Whitmore
1043 Rd 218
Cheyenne WY 82009

Call Sign: W7MEW
Michael E Whitmore
1043 Rd 218
Cheyenne WY 82009

Call Sign: KE7VWZ
Jeff R Baynard
951 Redhawk Dr
Cheyenne WY 82007

Call Sign: N7LOC
Jeanette A Curran
2812 Reed Ave
Cheyenne WY 82001

Call Sign: KJ7OJ
Ralph E Atchley
3061 Reed Ave No 3
Cheyenne WY 820012561

Call Sign: KC7CUW
James Espedido
1526 Reiner Pl
Cheyenne WY 82007

Call Sign: KB7SWR
Donnie M Smith
1526 Reiner Pl
Cheyenne WY 82007

Call Sign: KB7VQT
Jay D Smith
1526 Reiner Pl
Cheyenne WY 82007

Call Sign: KB7TDC
Katherine Smith
1526 Reiner Pl
Cheyenne WY 82007

Call Sign: N7SEY
Jay P Schiller
8614 Ridge Rd
Cheyenne WY 82009

Call Sign: KU2S
Raymond A Sirois Sr
5112 Ridge Rd
Cheyenne WY 82009

Call Sign: KC7OEQ
Deborah B Patton
7211 Rodeo Ct
Cheyenne WY 82009

Call Sign: KE7HUW
Ashley E Delong
1914 Rollins Ave
Cheyenne WY 82001

Call Sign: KE7DLG
Ronald J Delong
1914 Rollins Ave
Cheyenne WY 820014051

Call Sign: N7RJD
Ronald J Delong
1914 Rollins Ave
Cheyenne WY 820014051

Call Sign: KD7MBG
Thornton R Beaven
504 Roundup Rd
Cheyenne WY 82009

Call Sign: AC7XD
Thornton R Beaven
504 Roundup Rd
Cheyenne WY 82009

Call Sign: KQ6QY
Michael H Erlich Md
2114 Russell Ave
Cheyenne WY 820013928

Call Sign: KF6SGB
Stephanie S Erlich
2114 Russell Avenue
Cheyenne WY 820013928

Call Sign: KB7POY
Debby K Followell
2100 S 2nd Ave
Cheyenne WY 82007

Call Sign: N7REG
Eugene E Followell
2100 S 2nd Ave
Cheyenne WY 82007

Call Sign: KA0RBC
Barbara L Sahl
1719 S 4th Ave
Cheyenne WY 82007

Call Sign: N7YYF
Tony L Followell
1316 S Ahrens
Cheyenne WY 82007

Call Sign: KC7FQK
Stanley E Seidl Jr
1130 S Arp
Cheyenne WY 82007

Call Sign: KD0ZS
Charles M Felton
1115 S Greeley Hwy
Cheyenne WY 82007

Call Sign: KF7UNH
Ron E Goodner
2303 S Greeley Hwy
Cheyenne WY 82007

Call Sign: KF7CJG
Jerry W Bruce
S Greeley Hwy
Cheyenne WY 82007

Call Sign: NI7S
Charles E Charpentier
1903 S Greeley Hwy 179
Cheyenne WY 82007

Call Sign: KC7UUH
Tracy L Wallace
3400 S Greely Hwy 192
Cheyenne WY 82007

Call Sign: KD7SFS
Kyle R Knight
264 S Reed
Cheyenne WY 82007

Call Sign: KU7D
Warren R Appel
3917 Saddle Ridge Trl
Cheyenne WY 82001

Call Sign: WA7BSS
John F Nunley III
2508 Sagebrush Ave
Cheyenne WY 82009

Call Sign: KD7AN
Francis L Bumgarner
5311 Seslar Ave
Cheyenne WY 820094519

Call Sign: KA7MLO
Helen L Bumgarner
5311 Seslar Ave
Cheyenne WY 820094519

Call Sign: W7SQT
Bennie F James
804 Sevens Dr
Cheyenne WY 82001

Call Sign: KD7CLO
Leonard A Gordon
210 Seymour Ave
Cheyenne WY 82007

Call Sign: KE7RQE
April A Gordon
210 Seymour Ave
Cheyenne WY 82007

Call Sign: KE7RQC
Benjamin D Jacquot
3545 Shawnee St
Cheyenne WY 82001

Call Sign: N7CLV
James W Best
722 Shoshoni St
Cheyenne WY 82009

Call Sign: WU7G
James W Best
722 Shoshoni St
Cheyenne WY 82009

Call Sign: KC7FIM
Eric J Cortez
3531 Silvergate Dr
Cheyenne WY 82001

Call Sign: WY7FM
Eric J Cortez
3531 Silvergate Dr
Cheyenne WY 82001

Call Sign: W7WRO
Philip S Harris
3637 Silvergate Dr
Cheyenne WY 82001

Call Sign: W7COK
Ralph E Sims
2913 Sitting Bull
Cheyenne WY 82009

Call Sign: W7COJ
Lois B Sims
2913 Sitting Bull Rd
Cheyenne WY 820099620

Call Sign: KD7KAP
Christopher T Duncan
677 Snake River Ave
Cheyenne WY 82007

Call Sign: KE7LSU
Thomas Giordano
2922 Snyder Ave
Cheyenne WY 82001

Call Sign: KK7CU
Mark W Lockwood
1226 Sonata Ln
Cheyenne WY 82007

Call Sign: KC7WKB
Larry K Hobbs
709 Southfork Rd
Cheyenne WY 82007

Call Sign: N7WY
Robert W Rennard
1010 Spirit Ln
Cheyenne WY 820091856

Call Sign: KD7TND
John R Griffith
3112 Spruce Ct
Cheyenne WY 82001

Call Sign: WB4UIC
Thomas D Ritter
7916 Stagecoach Rd
Cheyenne WY 82009

Call Sign: KF6EYK
Kylle W Sheridan
3484 Stampede Ranch Rd
Cheyenne WY 82007

Call Sign: K9TCH
Gail F Sheridan
3484 Stampede Ranch Rd
Cheyenne WY 82007

Call Sign: W0SEV
Gail F Sheridan
3484 Stampede Ranch Rd
Cheyenne WY 82007

Call Sign: W7LES
Larry E Sheridan
3484 Stampede Ranch Rd
Cheyenne WY 82007

Call Sign: KC5NZV
Catherine C Gieser
1075 States Rd
Cheyenne WY 82009

Call Sign: KD5ACB
Elizabeth A Hollmann
1075 States Rd
Cheyenne WY 82009

Call Sign: KD5CYP
Matthew R Hollmann
1075 States Rd
Cheyenne WY 82009

Call Sign: KC5SGD
Sarah B Hollmann
1075 States Rd
Cheyenne WY 82009

Call Sign: KC5MUD
William J Hollmann
1075 States Rd
Cheyenne WY 82009

Call Sign: KC7DUY
Carol A Belongia
321 Stetson Dr
Cheyenne WY 82009

Call Sign: KA0OKX
Charlene L Rich
2200 Steve Ave
Cheyenne WY 82007

Call Sign: KB7T
Frank A Pascarelli
905 Stevens Dr
Cheyenne WY 82001

Call Sign: WE7MA
Martin A Luna
11412 Stewart Rd
Cheyenne WY 820099508

Call Sign: WA3WLV
Victor A Michael Jr
7901 Stoneridge Dr
Cheyenne WY 82009

Call Sign: KC7ISP
Edward C Carlson
1891 Studebaker
Cheyenne WY 82009

Call Sign: N0GNA
Raymond J Gomez Jr
4420 Sullivan
Cheyenne WY 82009

Call Sign: KC7ITD
Johan L Olsson
4303 Sullivan St
Cheyenne WY 82009

Call Sign: KC7KHG
Glen A Wagner
3114 Sun Rise Rd
Cheyenne WY 82001

Call Sign: AA7WQ
Carl E Dierks
3119 Sunrise Rd
Cheyenne WY 820016135

Call Sign: KB7ZWC
Christian M Winger
3413 Sunrise Rd
Cheyenne WY 82001

Call Sign: KC7KWN
Heidi G Winger
3413 Sunrise Rd
Cheyenne WY 82001

Call Sign: WY7UW
Mark J Winger
3413 Sunrise Rd
Cheyenne WY 82001

Call Sign: KF7CJJ
Brian C Rachocki
3526 Sunrise Rd
Cheyenne WY 82001

Call Sign: KF7GAZ
Lois M Rachocki
3526 Sunrise Rd
Cheyenne WY 82001

Call Sign: N7XMU
Larry G Christy
1626 Swing Dr
Cheyenne WY 82007

Call Sign: K7WYO
James S Uzzell
5163 Sycamore Rd
Cheyenne WY 82009

Call Sign: KD7PQS
James S Uzzell
5163 Sycamore Rd
Cheyenne WY 82009

Call Sign: KD7PUJ
Linda Uzzell
5163 Sycamore Rd
Cheyenne WY 82009

Call Sign: KD7PUK
Matt Uzzell
5163 Sycamore Rd
Cheyenne WY 82009

Call Sign: KD7WYO
Matt Uzzell
5163 Sycamore Rd
Cheyenne WY 82009

Call Sign: W7UZZ
Linda Uzzell
5163 Sycamore Rd
Cheyenne WY 82009

Call Sign: KD7SJR
Ruth A Uzzell
5163 Sycamore Rd
Cheyenne WY 82009

Call Sign: WT0F
Peter Ruble
5177 Sycamore Rd
Cheyenne WY 82009

Call Sign: AD7QN
Peter Ruble
5177 Sycamore Rd
Cheyenne WY 82009

Call Sign: W7ICU
David A Cromley
5603 Syracuse Rd
Cheyenne WY 82009

Call Sign: K6PRW
Glen A Parker
1001 Talbot Ct
Cheyenne WY 82001

Call Sign: KG6PRW
Glen A Parker
1001 Talbot Ct
Cheyenne WY 82001

Call Sign: KE7RQF
Dwight Hicks
1011 Talbot Ct
Cheyenne WY 82001

Call Sign: KA8ZWC
David E Thompson
925 Teresa Circle
Cheyenne WY 820091852

Call Sign: K7ALF
Alvin L Futch
1535 Terry Ranch Rd
Cheyenne WY 82007

Call Sign: KD7UGV
Alvin L Futch
1535 Terry Ranch Rd
Cheyenne WY 82007

Call Sign: KE7TWU
Neil B Brisbin
3008 Terry Rd 19
Cheyenne WY 82007

Call Sign: KD7LLJ
William R Culek
3008 Terry Rd 25
Cheyenne WY 82007

Call Sign: KD7LLF
Fredrick W Culek
3008 Terry Rd Sp 25
Cheyenne WY 82007

Call Sign: KE7UUD
Pamela K Vian
3008 Terry Rd Spc 25
Cheyenne WY 82007

Call Sign: KB7FTU
Hyrum S Shumway
3012 Thomes
Cheyenne WY 82001

Call Sign: KD0EQL
Frederick N Barton
2710 Thomes Ave Ste
1027
Cheyenne WY 82001

Call Sign: KD7VVE
Robert A Alexander
1042 Trails End Dr
Cheyenne WY 82009

Call Sign: N7LWH
Robert F Jacques
1828 Treadway Trl
Cheyenne WY 82009

Call Sign: N7VOL
Harley R Cleveland
107 Trinidad Ct
Cheyenne WY 82009

Call Sign: N7WMR
Lois K Cleveland
107 Trinidad Ct
Cheyenne WY 82009

Call Sign: N7EMA
H. Rob Cleveland
107 Trinidad Ct
Cheyenne WY 82009

Call Sign: WB7EMA
Aaron L Culver
121 Turk Ave
Cheyenne WY 82007

Call Sign: KB7VDL
Michael E Schutkowski
212 Tyler 35
Cheyenne WY 82007

Call Sign: KD7FPV
Michael C Stugelmayer
212 Tyler Pl 35

Cheyenne WY 82007

Call Sign: KD7LLG
Scott D Broadribb
1781 Ute Dr
Cheyenne WY 82005

Call Sign: N0BJB
Rex I Lewis
575 Valley View Dr
Cheyenne WY 82009

Call Sign: WL7CBM
Timothy B Lass
6508 Van Buren
Cheyenne WY 820093150

Call Sign: N7JUO
Steven L Spier
4501 Van Buren Ave
Cheyenne WY 82001

Call Sign: K7YM
Elmer W Ridcout Jr
6505 Van Buren Ave
Cheyenne WY 82009

Call Sign: WA7HQX
Kenneth D Andrews
719 Van Lennen
Cheyenne WY 820071505

Call Sign: K7HQX
Kenneth D Andrews
719 Van Lennen
Cheyenne WY 820071505

Call Sign: K7QGW
Harold R Duncan
807 Vandehei Ave
Cheyenne WY 82009

Call Sign: KC5PFA
Sylvia Steiger
1259 Ventnor Rd

Cheyenne WY 82009

Call Sign: KE7TWV
Daniel D Steiger
1259 Ventnor Rd
Cheyenne WY 82009

Call Sign: W7BZR
Jimmie A Hahn
910 W 10th St
Cheyenne WY 82007

Call Sign: W7AIE
Jimmie A Hahn
1314 W 18th St 13
Cheyenne WY 82001

Call Sign: KF7BFR
Laramie County
Emergency Management
310 W 19th St Ste 410
Cheyenne WY 82001

Call Sign: WY7EOC
Laramie County
Emergency Management
310 W 19th St Ste 410
Cheyenne WY 82001

Call Sign: KA7VIS
Joseph A Dolwick
1000 W 21st St
Cheyenne WY 82001

Call Sign: AC7W
Antoine J Oliger
1009 W 27th St
Cheyenne WY 82001

Call Sign: K7OWT
Bruce P Almich
215 W 28th St
Cheyenne WY 82001

Call Sign: KE7RQW

Donald W Day
213 W 2nd Ave
Cheyenne WY 82001

Call Sign: KD7FPU
Steven L Wagner
307 W 4th Ave
Cheyenne WY 82001

Call Sign: K7ARN
Robert M Arn
311 W 6th Ave
Cheyenne WY 82001

Call Sign: KD7PZQ
Robert M Arn
311 W 6th Ave
Cheyenne WY 82001

Call Sign: KF7CJA
Enoch D Johnson
619 W 6th St
Cheyenne WY 82007

Call Sign: N7ZAK
Roger W Kling
1054 W 6th St
Cheyenne WY 82007

Call Sign: K7DSK
Haskell C Cohen
411 W 7th Ave
Cheyenne WY 82001

Call Sign: N4HCJ
James L Kretzschmar
223 W 8th Ave
Cheyenne WY 82001

Call Sign: AE7AX
James L Kretzschmar
223 W 8th Ave
Cheyenne WY 82001

Call Sign: KF7CJF

Deborah A Kretzschmar
223 W 8th Ave
Cheyenne WY 82001

Call Sign: N7NBU
Judy L Nelson
425 W 8th Ave
Cheyenne WY 82001

Call Sign: N7ZWC
Thomas M De Hoff
630 W Dale Blvd
Cheyenne WY 82009

Call Sign: KB5YES
Kenneth L Purdes
5434 Walker Rd
Cheyenne WY 82009

Call Sign: WA9RCV
Jay A Nussbaum Sr
4804 Welchester Dr
Cheyenne WY 82009

Call Sign: KF7AFV
Linda A Cash
728 Western Hills Blvd
Cheyenne WY 82009

Call Sign: WB7RRZ
Wilson F Sellner
930 Western Hills Blvd
Cheyenne WY 820093323

Call Sign: WA7TJU
Larry E Langer
3102 Whitecloud Rd
Cheyenne WY 820016140

Call Sign: K1KLW
Kenneth L Watson
6950 Wild Bill Ct
Cheyenne WY 82001

Call Sign: KF7QFI

Kenneth L Watson
6950 Wild Bill Ct
Cheyenne WY 82001

Call Sign: KC7PFO
Ronald T Sherar
306 Williams
Cheyenne WY 82007

Call Sign: KC7VYW
Donna I Anders
417 Williams
Cheyenne WY 82007

Call Sign: KE7HGP
Ethan J Blooding
505 Williams 30
Cheyenne WY 82007

Call Sign: N7ZYX
Brad G Bush
505 Williams Spc 232
Cheyenne WY 82003

Call Sign: KC0ZHF
Rodney W Waln
402 Williams St
Cheyenne WY 82007

Call Sign: KC7UXI
Roseann J Ritter
4107 Wills Rd
Cheyenne WY 82001

Call Sign: KD7RJO
Brian T Lenell
5116 Windmill Rd
Cheyenne WY 82009

Call Sign: KD7SJQ
Amy J Lenell
5116 Windmill Rd
Cheyenne WY 82009

Call Sign: N2OFC

Cara C Moore
7418 Windsor Blvd
Cheyenne WY 82009

Call Sign: N7SDI
Patrick H Baird
7421 Windsor Blvd
Cheyenne WY 82009

Call Sign: KC7BQR
Sean P Baird
7421 Windsor Blvd
Cheyenne WY 82009

Call Sign: N7UFJ
Shari K Baird
7421 Windsor Blvd
Cheyenne WY 82009

Call Sign: KI4IB
Michael R Aurand
6517 Woods Rd
Cheyenne WY 82009

Call Sign: KD7MEJ
Norman R Hanson
6346 Yellowstone
Cheyenne WY 82009

Call Sign: WB7EOQ
Meade O Davis III
6020 Yellowstone Rd
Cheyenne WY 82009

Call Sign: KI7ZA
William F Dennis Jr
10114 Yellowstone Rd
Cheyenne WY 82009

Call Sign: WB7NEN
Arlene J Kensinger
11231 Yellowstone Rd
Cheyenne WY 82001

Call Sign: WB7CBF

Don C Kensinger
11231 Yellowstone Rd
Cheyenne WY 82009

Call Sign: KB5TWG
Anthony L Wadley
1933 Yuma Ct Unit B
Cheyenne WY 82001

Call Sign: KA7VGN
Jack L Butrick
Cheyenne WY 82003

Call Sign: WA1VPL
William V Daughtry Jr
Cheyenne WY 82003

Call Sign: N7UPE
Rodney J Drake
Cheyenne WY 82003

Call Sign: K7ANG
Paul J Preston
Cheyenne WY 82003

Call Sign: N6ULZ
David Allen
Cheyenne WY 82003

Call Sign: KD7IWQ
Leo J Bannon Jr
Cheyenne WY 820032138

Call Sign: WB7VNL
Raburn E Cahoon
Cheyenne WY 82001

Call Sign: KD5NAA
Cheryl G Chatham
Cheyenne WY 82003

Call Sign: KD5MZZ
Raymond P Chatham
Cheyenne WY 82003

Call Sign: KC7SHG
J Manuel Chavez
Cheyenne WY 82003

Call Sign: KD7RQV
Cynthia L Collister
Cheyenne WY 82003

Call Sign: W7YJG
Albert J De Bacco
Cheyenne WY 82003

Call Sign: KF7VR
Conrad T Dodson Jr
Cheyenne WY 82003

Call Sign: K7JEE
James E Elias
Cheyenne WY 82003

Call Sign: WR8O
Ronald J Gallo
Cheyenne WY 820037030

Call Sign: WA7KYM
Duane L Hansen
Cheyenne WY 82003

Call Sign: WA7BIL
Jon F Jacquot
Cheyenne WY 820037012

Call Sign: KA7SCL
Joyce D Johnston
Cheyenne WY 82003

Call Sign: KC7US
Luther R Johnston
Cheyenne WY 82003

Call Sign: KC7DHF
Robert E Knepper
Cheyenne WY 82003

Call Sign: KC0GDP

Russell R Lincoln
Cheyenne WY 82003

Call Sign: KD7GXU
Jason R Lyle Sr
Cheyenne WY 820032127

Call Sign: KD7JIZ
Sherrie A Lyle
Cheyenne WY 820032127

Call Sign: WB0TCZ
Martin E Mc Coy
Cheyenne WY 82003

Call Sign: KD5NWE
Pepper D Mcclenahan
Cheyenne WY 82003

Call Sign: KC7MGZ
Larry G Shafer
Cheyenne WY 82003

Call Sign: KC7SNO
Shy Wy Arc
Cheyenne WY 82003

Call Sign: KD7WGY
Shy-Wy Skywarn Team
Cheyenne WY 82003

Call Sign: KB7ZWE
John P Stewart
Cheyenne WY 82003

Call Sign: N0WRE
Peter E Summerhawk
Cheyenne WY 82004

Call Sign: KF7DFS
Daniel J Wilson
Cheyenne WY 82003

Call Sign: KF7UJI
David W Nelson

Cheyenne WY 82003

Call Sign: KE7RQD
Harlan R Ribnik
Cheyenne WY 82003

Call Sign: KE7JMZ
Henry A Snider Jr
Cheyenne WY 82003

Call Sign: K7CAS
Nicholas J Casner
Cheyenne WY 82003

Call Sign: WY2NJG
Sherrie A Lyle
Cheyenne WY 820032127

Call Sign: KF7CIX
Stephen L Green
Cheyenne WY 82003

FCC Amateur Radio Licenses in Chugwater

Call Sign: KC7DUX
Tom West
569 Ty Basin Rd
Chugwater WY
822100153

Call Sign: AD7CV
Tom West
569 Ty Basin Rd
Chugwater WY
822100153

Call Sign: KF7TCC
Ronald D Eicher
Chugwater WY 82210

FCC Amateur Radio Licenses in Clark

Call Sign: WB4QKZ

William J Garlough
175 Rd 8Ve
Clark WY 824358115

FCC Amateur Radio Licenses in Clearmont

Call Sign: AA7FR
David E Metcalf
4392 Hwy 14-16 E
Clearmont WY 82835

FCC Amateur Radio Licenses in Cody

Call Sign: KD7LTJ
Marie K Cook
2007 11th
Cody WY 82414

Call Sign: K0WY
Barron G Collier II
911 12th St
Cody WY 82414

Call Sign: KB5UCZ
Charles G Roudabush
937 13th St
Cody WY 82414

Call Sign: KD7RQY
Charles G Roudabush
937 13th St
Cody WY 82414

Call Sign: KA7ABY
David L Rodgers
1907 14th St
Cody WY 82414

Call Sign: KG4TRF
B Gathro
1108 14th St 184
Cody WY 82414

Call Sign: KD7FPQ
Ty G Wright
901 15th St
Cody WY 82414

Call Sign: KC7KTD
Roy F Epperle
1602.5 32nd St House A
Cody WY 82414

Call Sign: KC7MYY
Kathaleen A Epperle
1602.5 32nd St Hs A
Cody WY 82414

Call Sign: KC7NP
Allen R Hull Jr
1326 Alpine Ave
Cody WY 82414

Call Sign: KC7KTC
Carl R Shuler
80 Belfry Hwy
Cody WY 82414

Call Sign: K7MLH
Robert B Evans
2318 Big Horn Ave
Cody WY 82414

Call Sign: KC7AOB
Ronald K Morgan
2635 Big Horn Ave
Cody WY 82414

Call Sign: N6QYU
Linda Rae Sande
1219 Birch Ln
Cody WY 82414

Call Sign: KC7KJO
Everett B Jones
5 Black Heath Ct
Cody WY 82414

Call Sign: K7EBJ
Everett B Jones
5 Black Heath Ct
Cody WY 82414

Call Sign: WD4BDE
James E Elias
1120 Bleistein Avenue
Cody WY 82414

Call Sign: KB7YRG
Gail Knapp
23 Bow Blvd
Cody WY 82414

Call Sign: K7IKO
Lynn R Knapp
23 Bow Blvd
Cody WY 82414

Call Sign: KC7NVH
Cynthia M Moss Epperle
131 Buena Vista
Cody WY 82414

Call Sign: N7ODQ
Michael D Conners
201 Buena Vista Ave
Cody WY 82414

Call Sign: W7JBA
Connie J Ryan
2346 Carter Ave
Cody WY 82414

Call Sign: N7RLH
Robert W Brown
2402 Carter Ave
Cody WY 82414

Call Sign: KF7BJN
David C Hooper
3616 Cooper Ln
Cody WY 82414

Call Sign: KC7BND
Le Roy Morgan
4044 Cooper Ln
Cody WY 82414

Call Sign: KB7TRG
Mildred M Ross
15 Country Pl
Cody WY 82414

Call Sign: KE7TDG
Richard J Madsen
2616 Cowgill Rd
Cody WY 82414

Call Sign: KC7ISN
James L Atnip
39 CR 6Ss
Cody WY 82414

Call Sign: KC9IKH
Paul D Cooper
1531 Depot Dr
Cody WY 82414

Call Sign: KC7WWI
James F Dunkerley
440 Diamond Basin
Cody WY 82414

Call Sign: KF7LKR
Russell C Bingley
34 Gerber Ln
Cody WY 82414

Call Sign: N5ORF
Harold S Halvorsen
71 Green Creek Rd
Cody WY 82414

Call Sign: K7CWH
Charles W Harris
20 Hitching Post Dr
Cody WY 82414

Call Sign: KC6VPU
Charles W Harris
20 Hitching Post Dr
Cody WY 82414

Call Sign: KB7MXF
Jodell L Holder
4140 Hwy 14A
Cody WY 82414

Call Sign: KB7MXE
Justin E Holder
4140 Hwy 14A
Cody WY 82414

Call Sign: KC7QWS
Paul A Elliott
1907 Kerper Blvd
Cody WY 82414

Call Sign: KB7CQS
Martin J Zinn
2202 Kerper S
Cody WY 82414

Call Sign: KE7DMF
Springer T Rush Jr
26 Longhorn Dr
Cody WY 82414

Call Sign: K0GJ
Eric L Hill
5 Longhorn Dr
Cody WY 82414

Call Sign: KB6HAK
Judy L Morrow
8 Marquette Dr
Cody WY 82414

Call Sign: WB6DIJ
Robert J Morrow
8 Marquette Dr
Cody WY 82414

Call Sign: KF7DWZ
Ronald D Manley
122 Mccullough Dr
Cody WY 82414

Call Sign: KF7KHJ
Ruth J Manley
122 Mccullough Dr
Cody WY 82414

Call Sign: KB2OLM
Joseph F Ermer
15 Milo Rd
Cody WY 82414

Call Sign: NE7C
Paul M Rich
11 Musser Rd
Cody WY 82414

Call Sign: KE7SNM
Richard D Hall
215 N 44th St
Cody WY 82414

Call Sign: K4ZBP
John R Henthorn Jr
107 N Chugwater Dr
Cody WY 82414

Call Sign: KC7ILP
Elaine A Selby
3412 N Fork Hwy
Cody WY 82414

Call Sign: KB7ZPG
John A Mc Cue
1313 N Sunset Blvd
Cody WY 82414

Call Sign: NE7D
Patrick J Mc Cue
1313 N Sunset Blvd
Cody WY 82414

Call Sign: KA7UTW
Brad J Farmer
2562 Newton Ave
Cody WY 82414

Call Sign: W7NZI
Ivan Z Christopherson
61 Read 2Cd
Cody WY 82414

Call Sign: KF7RUB
Steven F Danforth
926 Stampede Ave
Cody WY 82414

Call Sign: KC8PLA
Edgar J Elliott
64 Nez Perce Dr
Cody WY 82414

Call Sign: KC7ISU
William H Giles
1201 Red Butte
Cody WY 82414

Call Sign: KD6NJJ
Judith L Tillery
14 Sunburst Dr
Cody WY 82414

Call Sign: W7STR
Springer T Rush Jr
732 Platinum Dr
Cody WY 82414

Call Sign: KC7ZAU
Bruce B Waters
1030 Red Butte Ave
Cody WY 82414

Call Sign: W7YWW
Floyd H Tillery
14 Sunburst Dr
Cody WY 82414

Call Sign: KB7CSV
Earl Holder
10 Poplar Rd
Cody WY 82414

Call Sign: KC7WDI
Travis W Waters
1030 Red Butte Ave
Cody WY 82414

Call Sign: KD7NZG
Willis Mcdonald IV
68 Sunset Rim
Cody WY 82414

Call Sign: KB7CSW
Justin E Holder
10 Poplar Rd
Cody WY 82414

Call Sign: N7AHK
Porter C Dalton
1213 Red Butte Ave
Cody WY 82414

Call Sign: KD7TKG
Lamont F Foster
17 Talon Dr
Cody WY 82414

Call Sign: W5JW
John G Webb
16 Ptarmigan Dr
Cody WY 82414

Call Sign: KD7USR
Krista L Wallace
249 Robert St
Cody WY 82414

Call Sign: N7DUS
Charles G Welch
33 Tanager Dr
Cody WY 82414

Call Sign: N7ZRM
Gracia R Christopherson
61 Rd 2 Cd
Cody WY 82414

Call Sign: KD7BKQ
E Vern Fales
1926 Shoshone Trl S
Cody WY 82414

Call Sign: KF6WIX
James E Fitzgerald Jr
2 Vista View Ln
Cody WY 824149606

Call Sign: AJ6H
Gerald R Hall
54 Rd 6 Km
Cody WY 824148020

Call Sign: WA2KRN
Walter Castle
119 Southfork Rd
Cody WY 82414

Call Sign: KF6WIW
Lynne M Fitzgerald
2 Vista View Ln
Cody WY 824149606

Call Sign: WD6CFN
Lillian M Hall
54 Rd 6 Km
Cody WY 824148020

Call Sign: NN1C
Deborah W Woodbridge
1789 Southfork Rd
Cody WY 82414

Call Sign: KF7DPQ
James E Fitzgerald Jr
2 Vista View Ln
Cody WY 824149606

Call Sign: KF7SKP
James E Fitzgerald Jr
2 Vista View Ln
Cody WY 824149606

Call Sign: KF7LYN
Lynne M Fitzgerald
2 Vista View Ln
Cody WY 824149606

Call Sign: WA7ITF
Ted J Ajax
18 Vista View Ln
Cody WY 82414

Call Sign: KC7PLJ
Sabrina J Kiele
109 W Yellowstone Ave
Cody WY 82414

Call Sign: W7PT
Phillip H Barnhart
Cody WY 82414

Call Sign: KI7W
Albert A Jaussaud
Cody WY 82414

Call Sign: K7ODE
Dannie R Shaffer
Cody WY 82414

Call Sign: KC7MNZ
Mary L Colling
Cody WY 824140215

Call Sign: KJ7QM
Steven J Colling
Cody WY 824140215

Call Sign: W7JIL
Eugene H Epperle Jr
Cody WY 82414

Call Sign: WA7UPK

Melba E Epperle
Cody WY 82414

Call Sign: KA8IZI
Marie A Szatkowski
Cody WY 82414

Call Sign: KF7DPN
James F Dunkerley Jr
Cody WY 82414

Call Sign: KB7CSX
Jodell L Justus
Cody WY 82414

Call Sign: KF7HCL
Jodell L Justus
Cody WY 82414

FCC Amateur Radio Licenses in Cokeville

Call Sign: KA7FQF
Ernest A Thornock
Box 5
Cokeville WY 83114

Call Sign: KC7JYT
Glenn L Birch
510 E Main
Cokeville WY 831140302

Call Sign: KE7OFM
William L Daniel
310 Pine St
Cokeville WY 83114

Call Sign: N7BRQ
John R Thornock
Cokeville WY 83114

Call Sign: KC7AAJ
Jason J Thornock
Cokeville WY 83114

Call Sign: KD7HRF
Ryan R Thornock
Cokeville WY 83114

Call Sign: K7CDY
Cody L Hollibaugh
Cokeville WY 83114

Call Sign: KE7PRU
Cody L Hollibaugh
Cokeville WY 83114

Call Sign: KD7VYE
Neil K Hymas
Cokeville WY 83114

Call Sign: KD7VYD
Ronald H Teichert
Cokeville WY 83114

FCC Amateur Radio Licenses in Cora

Call Sign: N7ATV
Woodrow M Wilson
Cora WY 82941

FCC Amateur Radio Licenses in Cowley

Call Sign: KC7UUR
Jerry W Warman
Cowley WY 82420

FCC Amateur Radio Licenses in Daniel

Call Sign: KC7ZTS
Burton A Bower
82 Pape Rd
Daniel WY 83115

FCC Amateur Radio Licenses in Dayton

Call Sign: N2SJS
Bernard P Daley
Dayton WY 828360189

Call Sign: N7XPL
Michael D Price
Dayton WY 828360157

Call Sign: NX0E
Christopher C Smith
Dayton WY 82836

Call Sign: KA7NNX
Susan K Smith
Dayton WY 82836

Call Sign: KF7PHO
Neil E Musilek
Dayton WY 82836

FCC Amateur Radio Licenses in Devils Tower

Call Sign: KE7ZHJ
North East Wy Contest Association
104 Hwy 24
Devils Tower WY 82714

Call Sign: KB7KRN
Lee Anne M Allen
82 Wenger Dr
Devils Tower WY 82714

Call Sign: KF7JPT
North East Wy Contest Association
82 Wenger Dr
Devils Tower WY 82714

Call Sign: W1KRB
Katie Allen
82 Wenger Dr
Devils Tower WY 82714

Call Sign: KB7JVO
Dwayne Allen
82 Wenger Rd
Devils Tower WY 82714

Call Sign: WY7DTW
Lee Anne M Sachau
Devils Tower WY 82714

FCC Amateur Radio Licenses in Diamondville

Call Sign: KC7OLR
Rocklyn N Hannah
307 Susie Ave
Diamondville WY 83116

Call Sign: N7ERH
Ronald K Bruderer
Diamondville WY 83116

Call Sign: KD7EMQ
Joan E Cederburg - Bruderer
Diamondville WY 831160522

Call Sign: K7JTP
Justin T Plowman
Diamondville WY 83116

Call Sign: KE7QVD
Justin T Plowman
Diamondville WY 83116

FCC Amateur Radio Licenses in Douglas

Call Sign: KI0KD
Michael J Lewis
36 1st St Orin
Douglas WY 82633

Call Sign: KD7PVI

Sherry E Snow
36 1st St Orin
Douglas WY 82633

Call Sign: NG7L
Dan M Arnold
275 Bar Two Dr
Douglas WY 82633

Call Sign: N7XKU
Jill R Arnold
275 Bar Two Dr
Douglas WY 82633

Call Sign: KC7UOP
Don E Gushurst
320 Chalk Buttes Rd
Douglas WY 82633

Call Sign: KE7VIB
Ian D Robertson
525 Cold Springs Rd
Douglas WY 82633

Call Sign: N7RQU
Fred A Teal Jr
412 Irvine Rd
Douglas WY 82633

Call Sign: K1FAT
Fred A Teal Jr
412 Irvine Rd
Douglas WY 82633

Call Sign: WB7AEM
Richard W Marler
421 N 2nd St
Douglas WY 82633

Call Sign: N7GSW
Dianne J France
719 S 10th St
Douglas WY 82633

Call Sign: W7OGT

Keith C France
719 S 10th St
Douglas WY 82633

Call Sign: WA0ZZU
Franklin M Prohaska
527 S 7th St
Douglas WY 82633

Call Sign: KB6VGS
Kenneth J Bollinger
42 Sierra
Douglas WY 82633

Call Sign: KF7PTK
Kenneth J Bollinger
42 Sierra
Douglas WY 82633

Call Sign: KE7NPB
William L De Rycke
31 Sunflower Trl
Douglas WY 82633

Call Sign: KD7GQO
Jill C Erickson
624 Van Buren
Douglas WY 82633

Call Sign: N7PTQ
Kent C Erickson
624 Van Buren
Douglas WY 82633

Call Sign: KC7CTY
Andie L Fink
756 Wagonhound Rd
Douglas WY 82633

Call Sign: KI7XH
Darrin L Fink
756 Wagonhound Rd
Douglas WY 82633

Call Sign: KB7ZJS

Edward G Leonard
Douglas WY 82633

Call Sign: KI7TG
David L Yearout
Douglas WY 82633

Call Sign: WA0DRG
Earle G Fetterman
Douglas WY 82633

Call Sign: N7KOH
Fredrick D Kilmer
Douglas WY 82633

Call Sign: KD5HQM
Donald E Norvell
Douglas WY 826330560

Call Sign: KB5TGX
Julia L Norvell
Douglas WY 826330560

Call Sign: N5WGX
Morris E Norvell
Douglas WY 82633

Call Sign: KK7BA
Gordon A Smith
Douglas WY 82633

FCC Amateur Radio Licenses in Dubois

Call Sign: N7UOH
Wendy S Kuhlman
Box 374
Dubois WY 82513

Call Sign: KB7RCM
Greg L Stone
Box 422
Dubois WY 82513

Call Sign: K0FRN

Sammy J Christensen
304 Horse Creek Rd
Dubois WY 82513

Call Sign: KB7PLB
Arlene A Dyess
644 Mountain View Dr
Dubois WY 82513

Call Sign: KB7PLC
Keri A Dyess
644 Mountain View Dr
Dubois WY 82513

Call Sign: N7TZI
Wayne L Dyess
644 Mt View Dr
Dubois WY 82513

Call Sign: KE7GDF
Joseph W Mc Intire
27 Riverview Dr
Dubois WY 82513

Call Sign: KG6JIY
Harold B Marcotte
10 Warm Springs Rd
Dubois WY 82513

Call Sign: KD7IDM
Edwin D Covell
Dubois WY 82513

Call Sign: K7ACM
Michael W Davis
Dubois WY 82513

Call Sign: WB7PZP
Bonnie C Kuhlman
Dubois WY 82513

Call Sign: WB7FIU
Edward J Kuhlman
Dubois WY 82513

Call Sign: WB7CBQ
Stephen E Powell
Dubois WY 82513

Call Sign: KF7MDR
Boyd W Brown
Dubois WY 82513

Call Sign: KF7HID
John G Muhlenkamp III
Dubois WY 82513

Call Sign: KF7DMF
Radawna K Kuhlman
Dubois WY 82513

FCC Amateur Radio Licenses in Elk Mountain

Call Sign: K7PPC
Robert K Meyer
Box 57
Elk Mountain WY 82324

FCC Amateur Radio Licenses in Emblem

Call Sign: KE7HH
David O Neves
3360 Rd 12
Emblem WY 82422

FCC Amateur Radio Licenses in Encampment

Call Sign: W7LQY
Leonard H Clark
820 Barnett Ave
Encampment WY 82325

Call Sign: W4MCZ
Richard A Williams
208 Dillon Ave
Encampment WY 82325

Call Sign: KC4KQA
Ellen M Klinefelter
217 Mc Caffery
Encampment WY 82325

Call Sign: N0TGZ
Alan C Braga
Encampment WY
823250097

Call Sign: K2AME
William W Dudan
Encampment WY 82325

Call Sign: N0VRA
Jerry L Westerfield
Encampment WY 82325

Call Sign: KE7OPP
James F Johnson
Encampment WY 82325

Call Sign: K7AME
William W Dudan
Encampment WY 82325

FCC Amateur Radio Licenses in Etna

Call Sign: KD7HMV
Holly P Bateman
174 Etna Forest Rd
Etna WY 83118

Call Sign: KD7HMW
John D Bateman
174 Etna Forest Rd
Etna WY 83118

Call Sign: K7PDQ
Wendell D Warren
243 Etna W
Etna WY 83118

Call Sign: WB7UBV

Teresa L Laker
Mi N
Etna WY 831185074

Call Sign: WB7EUT
Craig M Laker
Mile N
Etna WY 831185074

Call Sign: W6EXY
John F Flagg
111 Quaking Aspen Way
Etna WY 83118

Call Sign: KA6SQD
Dean Arthur Carey
Etna WY 83118

Call Sign: KC5DII
Sarah N Collins
Etna WY 83118

Call Sign: KC7OKJ
John C Roberts
Etna WY 83118

Call Sign: KD7BUV
Marc A Speth
Etna WY 83118

Call Sign: KE7QPM
Benjamin J Randall
Etna WY 83118

Call Sign: KE7QPN
John J Randall
Etna WY 83118

Call Sign: KF7QEW
Travis J Martin
Etna WY 83118

FCC Amateur Radio Licenses in Evanston

Call Sign: KB7WZW
Trevor K Pfaff
324 15th St
Evanston WY 82930

Call Sign: KJ4QHZ
Lawrence W Holmes
435 6th St
Evanston WY 82930

Call Sign: KF7SLZ
Brian C Woodward
3047 Almy Rd 107
Evanston WY 82930

Call Sign: WO0DY
Brian C Woodward
3047 Almy Rd 107
Evanston WY 82930

Call Sign: KB7EAS
Joe D Espinoza
333 Arrowhead Dr
Evanston WY 82930

Call Sign: N7YOK
Robert R Rintoul
Box 79G
Evanston WY 82930

Call Sign: N6QFQ
Scott A Greer
207 Broken Circle Dr
Evanston WY 82930

Call Sign: KF7TXM
Michael J D'Anzi
446 Center St
Evanston WY 82930

Call Sign: KB7VSA
Jeremy J Conk
122 Citation Ln
Evanston WY 82930

Call Sign: N7LMN
Robin L Conk
122 Citation Ln
Evanston WY 82930

Call Sign: KA7AHB
Janice M Albert
54 City View Dr
Evanston WY 82930

Call Sign: KA7AHA
Paul W Albert
54 City View Dr
Evanston WY 82930

Call Sign: N7RLF
Steven L Lofthouse
262 City View Dr
Evanston WY 82930

Call Sign: KD7GLK
Paul D Rasmussen Jr
150 Constitution Ave Apt
2
Evanston WY 82930

Call Sign: WB7QID
Wayne L Bollschweiler
204 CR
Evanston WY 829302548

Call Sign: KA7VMI
Melissa Davis
212 CR
Evanston WY 82930

Call Sign: KD7BAV
Daniel S Vansyoc
2038 CR 173
Evanston WY 82930

Call Sign: KB7RAP
Steve A Lester
3010 CR 173
Evanston WY 82930

Call Sign: KB7VLS
Michael K Green
205 Dean Ave
Evanston WY 82930

Call Sign: N7TYF
Jefferson D Stacy
140 Del Rio Dr
Evanston WY 82930

Call Sign: N7VSD
Robert W Bryan
105 Evans Ln
Evanston WY 82930

Call Sign: KF7QBY
Natalie M Paddock
105 Fox Point Ct
Evanston WY 82930

Call Sign: KF7XM
Vernon D Cole
61 Grass Valley Dr
Evanston WY 82930

Call Sign: KB7ZU
Randy M Erickson
431 Hathaway Ave
Evanston WY 82930

Call Sign: N7YOJ
Theron L Hutchinson
14001 Hwy 150 S
Evanston WY 82930

Call Sign: N7SIB
Charles W Crompton
1831 Hwy 89 N
Evanston WY 82930

Call Sign: KC5GBI
Glen Huling
436 Laramie Dr
Evanston WY 82930

Call Sign: KC7SMR
J Ryan Corbett
105 Mountain Village Rd
Evanston WY 82930

Call Sign: KD7ONP
Edward M Huber
114 Mt Village Rd Apt D
Evanston WY 82930

Call Sign: WA7MEK
David J Smith
57 Patriot Ct
Evanston WY 82930

Call Sign: N7HCH
Lawrence K Edrington
116 Piper Ct
Evanston WY 829305418

Call Sign: KB6OUO
Maria E P Johnson
167 Rapid Canyon Rd
Evanston WY 82930

Call Sign: N7YOE
Leah A Jones Jr
116 Sherman Way
Evanston WY 82930

Call Sign: N7YOG
Roy F Jones
116 Sherman Way
Evanston WY 82930

Call Sign: N5ZGG
Wendell C Webb
Silver Sage Dr
Evanston WY 82930

Call Sign: WA7ED
Edward M Huber
757 Sioux Dr
Evanston WY 829304551

Call Sign: N7YOF
Richard G Timperley
800 Sixth St
Evanston WY 82930

Call Sign: KC7EON
Jayson W Maples
13699 So Hwy 150
Evanston WY 82930

Call Sign: N7LNY
Michael A Corder
631 Stahley
Evanston WY 82930

Call Sign: KA0RLO
Susan J Corder
631 Stahley Ave
Evanston WY 829305121

Call Sign: N7XD
Terence A Davis
1849 W Anderson
Evanston WY 82930

Call Sign: N7DT
Clarence J Vranish
1912 W Anderson
Evanston WY 82930

Call Sign: N7SMM
Michael L Vranish
1912 W Anderson
Evanston WY 82930

Call Sign: N7QWZ
K Quinn Hanks
205 Washakie Dr
Evanston WY 82930

Call Sign: N7QWY
Kenneth E Hanks
205 Washakie Dr
Evanston WY 82930

Call Sign: N7QXA
Troy D Hanks
205 Washakie Dr
Evanston WY 82930

Call Sign: W7PCF
Paul C Fry
233 Woodridge Ln
Evanston WY 82930

Call Sign: KB7MZK
David L Runyan
178 Yellow Creek Rd Apt
F
Evanston WY 82930

Call Sign: KI7DC
Quintan R Bonner
Evanston WY 82931

FCC Amateur Radio Licenses in Evansville

Call Sign: KC7LQB
Thomas K Sherwin
Box 673
Evansville WY 826360673

Call Sign: WA2SMS
Steven M Strauss
9076 E Turquoise Rd
Evansville WY 826369792

Call Sign: N7YVL
Vincent L Yankey
384 Holmes St
Evansville WY 82636

Call Sign: KC7JHV
Keith W Humphrey
236 Missouri St
Evansville WY 82636

Call Sign: KE7QF

David E Reynolds
980 Park Ln
Evansville WY 826369538

Call Sign: KD7QVM
Ihla M Jennewein
250 Roundup Rd
Evansville WY 82636

Call Sign: KD7PIC
Basil C Petumenos
250 Roundup Rd
Evansville WY 82636

Call Sign: K7HBB
Harold H Clay
Evansville WY 82636

Call Sign: N7SDW
Elizabeth S Wells
Evansville WY 82636

Call Sign: KC7MJJ
Steven R Hunt
Evansville WY 82636

Call Sign: N7AOK
Ralph D Johnson
Evansville WY 82636

Call Sign: KC8JSC
Jeffrey A Moore
Evansville WY 826360311

Call Sign: KD7RX
Jerry Sherwin
Evansville WY 826360673

Call Sign: KD7NHK
Cory L Vogt
Evansville WY 82636

Call Sign: KE4RXM
Tom Waters
Evansville WY 826360312

Call Sign: KE7ZCQ
Charles G Breed
Evansville WY 82636

Call Sign: KF7GNC
Cory W Pritchard
Evansville WY 82636

Call Sign: KE7WQP
Michael L Bond
Evansville WY 82636

FCC Amateur Radio Licenses in Fairview

Call Sign: KC2QCK
Robert Young
2825 Spring Creek Rd
Fairview WY 83119

FCC Amateur Radio Licenses in Farson

Call Sign: N6IGC
Bennie G Hicks
Farson WY 829320117

FCC Amateur Radio Licenses in FE Warren AFB

Call Sign: KB7JSB
Robert G Burns
Minuteman Dr
FE Warren AFB WY
82001

Call Sign: WB6COP
Joshua A Thomas
6111 Randall Ave
FE Warren AFB WY
82005

FCC Amateur Radio Licenses in Fort Bridger

Call Sign: KF7RVL
J Thad Stevens
1441 CR 217
Fort Bridger WY 82933

Call Sign: KD7AUQ
Robert B Adams
3242 CR 217
Fort Bridger WY 82933

Call Sign: KF7ELU
Clayton D Lowther
Fort Bridger WY 82933

FCC Amateur Radio Licenses in Freedom

Call Sign: KB7RAR
Jill Hubbard
20 Cedar Creek CR 118
Freedom WY 83120

Call Sign: KC7VXJ
Corey N Pantuso
6858 Hwy 34
Freedom WY 83120

Call Sign: KD7LKO
Bonnie B Pantuso
Freedom WY 83120

FCC Amateur Radio Licenses in Gillette

Call Sign: KE7TWE
Krista L Thompson
3312 Alberta Dr
Gillette WY 82718

Call Sign: N0WQ
Lee A Jorgensen
4411 Alison Ave

Gillette WY 82717   Gillette WY 82716   Gillette WY 827187174

Call Sign: KB7SSM   Call Sign: AD7KI   Call Sign: N7YJI
Jody G Telkamp   Delmer L Howery Jr   David B Patterson
1109 Almon Cir   1507 Boise Ave   8130 Chukar Dr
Gillette WY 82716   Gillette WY 82716   Gillette WY 82716

Call Sign: WA6ELO   Call Sign: KF7CBC   Call Sign: KE7TG
V Frank Goodwin Jr   Hailee A Howery   Christine M Bingham
64 Alpine Dr   1507 Boise Ave   3310 Crestline Cir
Gillette WY 827188821   Gillette WY 82716   Gillette WY 82716

Call Sign: WB6EQH   Call Sign: N7XUF   Call Sign: KE7NT
L Jane Goodwin   Janette C Collins   Leo C Bingham
64 Alpine Dr   Box 309   3310 Crestline Cir
Gillette WY 827188821   Gillette WY 82717   Gillette WY 82716

Call Sign: KA7AJB   Call Sign: KC7RJ   Call Sign: KF7DLT
Richard J Bell   Kevin P Collins   Chirs L Huber
2551 Antler Rd   Box 309   110 Daly Rd
Gillette WY 82718   Gillette WY 82717   Gillette WY 82716

Call Sign: N7XKT   Call Sign: KC7CXZ   Call Sign: KB7TGR
Garth L Crowe Sr   Dieter G Awiszus   Jim A Backer
1206 Avalon Ct   4908 Brahma   8 Dawn Dr
Gillette WY 827165202   Gillette WY 82718   Gillette WY 82716

Call Sign: KD5HTJ   Call Sign: KC7UBR   Call Sign: KE7TWF
Rhea Ann Crowe   Michael R Doherty   Elaine K Backer
1206 Avalon Ct   2720 Cascade Ct   8 Dawn Dr
Gillette WY 82716   Gillette WY 82718   Gillette WY 82716

Call Sign: KF7STJ   Call Sign: KC7VYX   Call Sign: KF7GSA
Wade B Watson   Robert N Madsen   John W Butler Jr
690 Bell Rd   816 Cherry Ln   1001 Desert Hill Apt 40
Gillette WY 82718   Gillette WY 82716   Gillette WY 82717

Call Sign: W7WBW   Call Sign: KD7QDP   Call Sign: N7XUG
Wade B Watson   Richard E Benedict   Richard D Wolf
690 Bell Rd   7730 Chukar   2602 Dogwood Ave
Gillette WY 82718   Gillette WY 82718   Gillette WY 827186302

Call Sign: KD6UBK   Call Sign: KD7QDO   Call Sign: NE7WY
Delmer L Howery Jr   Cheryl K Benedict   Northeast Wyoming
1507 Boise Ave   7730 Chukar Dr   Amateur Radio Assn

2816 Dogwood Ave
Gillette WY 82718

Call Sign: WY7WST
Inc. North East Wyoming
Amateur Radio Associatin
2816 Dogwood Ave
Gillette WY 82718

Call Sign: WY7CAM
Inc. North East Wyoming
Amateur Radio
Association
2816 Dogwood Ave
Gillette WY 82718

Call Sign: WY7CRK
Inc. North East Wyoming
Amateur Radio
Association
2816 Dogwood Ave
Gillette WY 82718

Call Sign: KE7ZHS
Inc. North East Wyoming
Amateur Radio
Association
501 Douglas Hwy Ste A
Gillette WY 82716

Call Sign: KB7UNA
Bobby E Fletcher
1401 E 12th 1
Gillette WY 82716

Call Sign: KE7OSF
Justin M Cody
1120 E 12th St
Gillette WY 82716

Call Sign: WA7TAY
Elton E Smith
1116 E 9th St
Gillette WY 82716

Call Sign: KF7DLS
Shane A Warner
820 E Laramie St Apt E
Gillette WY 82716

Call Sign: NE7EK
Anthony E Kyriss
400 E Third Avenue
Gillette WY 82716

Call Sign: K7RDC
Chad A Cundy
311 E Walnut
Gillette WY 82718

Call Sign: K7EMR
Robert Underwood
3201 Echeta Rd 79
Gillette WY 82716

Call Sign: K4EMR
Donna M Underwood
3201 Echeta Rd 79
Gillette WY 82716

Call Sign: KB7QAO
Christopher S Rigsby
3201 Echeta Rd 105
Gillette WY 82716

Call Sign: KF7LFQ
Scott E Campbell
1008 Elon St Apt D
Gillette WY 82716

Call Sign: KE7KBF
Gary S Horlick
5 Emerald Ave
Gillette WY 82716

Call Sign: W7GSH
Gary S Horlick
5 Emerald Ave
Gillette WY 82716

Call Sign: N0VVT
Andy J Strand
3211 Foothills Blvd
Gillette WY 82716

Call Sign: KD7ICJ
Don D Duncan
3513 Foothills Blvd
Gillette WY 82716

Call Sign: KB7ZKG
Rodney C Erickson
3730 Foothills Blvd
Gillette WY 82716

Call Sign: KC7YQZ
Matthew G Case
501 Granite
Gillette WY 82718

Call Sign: KA7WYF
Benjamin D Mitchell
1205 Green Ave 111
Gillette WY 82716

Call Sign: KC7ZVU
Troy A Cormaney
806 Greenway B
Gillette WY 82716

Call Sign: KA7ZZB
Darrel A Layton
5600 Hannum Rd 15
Gillette WY 827161451

Call Sign: KF7CBE
Lucille M Layton
5600 Hannum Rd Lot 15
Gillette WY 82716

Call Sign: WR7CW
Earl J Welter
4402 Hi Line Rd
Gillette WY 827188268

Call Sign: KJ5HE
Earl J Welter
4402 Hi Line Rd
Gillette WY 827188268

Call Sign: KD7JY
Charles W Burns
3700 Hidden Valley
Gillette WY 82716

Call Sign: KD7ZUQ
James W Greer Jr
3707 Hidden Valley Rd
Gillette WY 82718

Call Sign: KK7NI
Earl J Welter
4402 Hiline Rd
Gillette WY 827174241

Call Sign: KD7ATY
Mikkael J Chick
6511 Irving Blvd
Gillette WY 82718

Call Sign: KB7HVD
Roland E Miller
3305 Kinner Dr
Gillette WY 82718

Call Sign: KF7CBB
Chris M Eslinger
2706 Kirk Ct
Gillette WY 82718

Call Sign: KC7NGO
Leda M Pojman
2402 Knollwood
Gillette WY 82718

Call Sign: N7GQC
Fokke M Gerrits
2410 Knollwood Dr
Gillette WY 82716

Call Sign: AC7OK
Jerry L Boyett
1411 Lobo Ln
Gillette WY 82718

Call Sign: N7LHI
Jerry L Boyett
1411 Lobo Ln
Gillette WY 82718

Call Sign: K7TNT
Richard L Harrod
4108 Longhorn Ave
Gillette WY 82718

Call Sign: AL7NI
Ronald G Kline
1900 Meadow Ln
Gillette WY 82718

Call Sign: N7VWY
Terrence L O Brien
2703 Meadow Ln
Gillette WY 82716

Call Sign: W7TNJ
Wilford T Bell
1410 Michelle St
Gillette WY 82718

Call Sign: N7VWW
Thomas F Early
5004 Milton Hcr 81
Gillette WY 82716

Call Sign: K7HPL
John W Tieman
1603 Monte Vista Ln
Gillette WY 82716

Call Sign: N7YBF
Lester C Hecht
1209 N Rawhide Dr
Gillette WY 82716

Call Sign: KC7MUH
Shirley A Hecht
1209 N Rawhide Dr
Gillette WY 82716

Call Sign: N7PCC
Loren E Hyde
1 Navajo Cir
Gillette WY 82716

Call Sign: KC0RAG
Chris M Hoy
1300 Orchid Ln
Gillette WY 82716

Call Sign: KC7JPI
Matthew L Love Sr
4 Peak Court
Gillette WY 827162265

Call Sign: KA0JEL
Donald A Morrison
1405 Preamble Ln
Gillette WY 82716

Call Sign: WU7Y
William S Edwards
8200 Ramshorn Dr
Gillette WY 82718

Call Sign: W7HNI
Arlen D Gaddis
210 Richards
Gillette WY 82716

Call Sign: KF7CBH
Harold W Howells
701 Richards Ave
Gillette WY 82717

Call Sign: WG7Z
Randall A Schaefer
7701 Robin Dr
Gillette WY 82718

Call Sign: AA7AQ
Steven J Schaefer
7701 Robin Dr
Gillette WY 82716

Call Sign: N7ZRO
Clint L Copping
605 Rockpile Blvd
Gillette WY 82716

Call Sign: KB7QAP
Patricia N Eekhoff
808 Rodeo
Gillette WY 82716

Call Sign: N7VWU
Thomas J Eekhoff
808 Rodeo
Gillette WY 82716

Call Sign: KC7GOV
Jeremy P Maslak
2213 Rose Creek Dr
Gillette WY 82718

Call Sign: N7QMX
Rodney W Warne
2401 Rose Creek Dr
Gillette WY 82716

Call Sign: KE7QVO
John H Fischer
501 S Douglas Hwy
Gillette WY 82716

Call Sign: KE7ZHT
Inc. North East Wyoming
Amateur Radio Associatin
501 S Douglas Hwy Ste A
Gillette WY 82716

Call Sign: KE7EKB
Joseph A Trujillo
2610 S Douglas Hwy Ste
180 524

Gillette WY 82718

Call Sign: KD7AMP
Brenda K Uppling
2610 S Douglas Hwy Ste
180 536
Gillette WY 82718

Call Sign: W5WIB
John G Uppling Jr
2610 S Douglas Hwy Ste
180 536
Gillette WY 82718

Call Sign: KE7ZHU
Inc. North East Wyoming
Amateur Radio
Association
501 S Douglas Hwy Ste A
Gillette WY 82716

Call Sign: K7KAS
John G Uppling Jr
501 S Douglas Hwy Ste A
Gillette WY 82716

Call Sign: K7CAN
John G Uppling Jr
501 S Douglas Hwy Ste A
Gillette WY 82718

Call Sign: N7QAX
William V Torrance
600 S Garner Lake Rd 80
Gillette WY 82718

Call Sign: KE7TWG
Robert E Avery
606 S Osborne Ave
Gillette WY 82716

Call Sign: W7REA
Robert E Avery
606 S Osborne Ave
Gillette WY 82716

Call Sign: KD7EHG
Robert A Wells
2700 Sammye Ave
Gillette WY 82718

Call Sign: KF7AMV
Gayle R Wells
2700 Sammye Ave
Gillette WY 82718

Call Sign: N7QMP
Gilbert S Rauscher
252 Sierra Cir
Gillette WY 82716

Call Sign: N7MKW
Thomas J Henaghan
703 Stanley Ave
Gillette WY 82716

Call Sign: KD7JOF
William B Woodward III
5601 Stone Trl
Gillette WY 82718

Call Sign: W7DOC
William B Woodward Jr
5601 Stone Trl Ave
Gillette WY 827184057

Call Sign: KC7UBS
Daniel C Mitchell
4311 Tanner Dr
Gillette WY 82718

Call Sign: KF7CBD
Jeff A Bryant
4001 Tepee St
Gillette WY 82718

Call Sign: N7XPJ
Lawrence P Cisneros
1049 Teton Cir
Gillette WY 82716

Call Sign: KE7PYF
Bryan M Shannon
3801 Triton Avenue
Gillette WY 82718

Call Sign: KE7EKA
David A King
401 W 10th St
Gillette WY 82716

Call Sign: WY7DK
David A King
401 W 10th St
Gillette WY 82716

Call Sign: WY7GC
Gillette Campus Science
Club
720 W 8th St NW
Gillette WY 82716

Call Sign: KD7RVU
Kirk L Jacobson
204 W Boxelder
Gillette WY 82718

Call Sign: KC7HFQ
Lloyd E Stewart
410 W Boxelder Rd
Gillette WY 82718

Call Sign: K0DYJ
Justin M Cody
302 W Tonk St
Gillette WY 82718

Call Sign: KC7CYA
Larry D Mc Eachron
802 W Warlow Dr 8
Gillette WY 82716

Call Sign: WG7Y
Robert E Davis
1010 Warren Ave

Gillette WY 82716

Call Sign: KF7CBF
Joan B Davis
1010 Warren Ave
Gillette WY 82716

Call Sign: WY7JOD
Joan B Davis
1010 Warren Ave
Gillette WY 82716

Call Sign: KD7IYX
Jeffrey L Miller
3230 Watsabaugh Dr
Gillette WY 82718

Call Sign: KC8RCF
Nathan L Bookwalter
55 Willow Lake Rd
Gillette WY 82716

Call Sign: KE7NPC
Timothy D Slattery
37 Willow St
Gillette WY 82716

Call Sign: WD0ENC
Wayne C Lindgren
1690 Wolff Rd
Gillette WY 82718

Call Sign: N7XUE
Bernie A Damori
Gillette WY 82717

Call Sign: KD7IUL
Contest Cowboys Arc
Gillette WY 82717

Call Sign: KD7RDC
Chad A Cundy
Gillette WY 827170853

Call Sign: KB7FIE

Darryl W Lenz
Gillette WY 82716

Call Sign: KC7CXY
Debra A Lindgren
Gillette WY 82717

Call Sign: KJ7UG
Robert E Martin Jr
Gillette WY 827171204

Call Sign: KB7PTH
William W Reed
Gillette WY 82717

Call Sign: KD7JEO
Preston W Schilling
Gillette WY 82717

Call Sign: KC7FXD
Glenn A Sutherland
Gillette WY 82717

Call Sign: KA0RKL
Michael D Wenz
Gillette WY 82717

Call Sign: KD7JFU
Nicholas R Wright
Gillette WY 82717

Call Sign: KE7ZHV
Christine A Butler
Gillette WY 82717

Call Sign: KE7MXN
David E Kelsay
Gillette WY 827174276

Call Sign: N1CKW
Nicholas R Wright
Gillette WY 82717

Call Sign: KF7GRZ
Stering C Davis

Gillette WY 82717

Call Sign: K7NQX
Glen R Blackburn
505 3rd St
Glendo WY 822130021

Call Sign: N7ELE
Allen W Haygood
111 S Lincoln
Glendo WY 82213

Call Sign: KA7PNH
William W Blackburn
144 Boxelder Rd
Glenrock WY 82637

Call Sign: KD0VK
Alvin W Schmoldt
803 Grant
Glenrock WY 826371976

Call Sign: KE6SCM
Lionel D Courselle
927 Keller Dr
Glenrock WY 82637

Call Sign: WA7CON
Joseph C Delwiche
35 Mesa Verde Dr
Glenrock WY 82637

Call Sign: KV7G
Maurice L Haynes
216 N 3rd St
Glenrock WY 82637

Call Sign: N7EID
Maxine E Haynes

216 N 3rd St
Glenrock WY 82637

Call Sign: WB7RDH
Robert N Maines
109 N Monkey
Glenrock WY 82637

Call Sign: N7DLU
Timothy R Grenseman
92 So Monkey Rd
Glenrock WY 82637

Call Sign: KF7CFX
Charles L Lyford
Glenrock WY 82637

Call Sign: KF7CFW
Joyce I Lyford
Glenrock WY 82637

Call Sign: KY7Q
Richard S Oakley
521 Chimney Rock Loop
Granite Canon WY 82059

Call Sign: KF7CJI
John E Sutherland
642 I80 Service Rd
Granite Canon WY 82059

Call Sign: KF7CJH
Aleta M Sutherland
642 Interstate 80
Granite Canon WY 82059

Call Sign: KF7PDP
Joshua W Coursey

2695 Alamosa Circle
Green River WY 82935

Call Sign: KE7FGD
Judy K Roderick
409 Andrews
Green River WY 82935

Call Sign: KD7HOX
John P Montz Sr
2220 Colorado Dr
Green River WY
829356106

Call Sign: N8WRF
Donald E Wright
15 E 3rd North St
Green River WY 82935

Call Sign: N0NBC
Dale W Arey
650 Easy St
Green River WY
829354909

Call Sign: W7NBC
Dale W Arey
650 Easy St
Green River WY
829354909

Call Sign: NW7I
Roger N Nielsen
350 Fir
Green River WY 82935

Call Sign: WY7UPR
Christopher J Pritchard
325 Greasewood
Green River WY 82935

Call Sign: KK7SG
Patrick J Nicholson
295 Hackberry St
Green River WY 82935

Call Sign: N7IHO
Roger J Veys
2640 Hawaii Ct
Green River WY 82935

Call Sign: KE7FGC
Ethan D Slaton
2025 Iowa Circle
Green River WY 82935

Call Sign: KE7FGB
Stephen R Slaton
2025 Iowa Circle
Green River WY 82935

Call Sign: KB7HOX
Jeffrey V Nieters
1115 Kentucky St
Green River WY 82935

Call Sign: KB7HOY
Patricia A Nieters
1115 Kentucky St
Green River WY 82935

Call Sign: KB7ZLS
Taylor Q Vu
910 Kit Carson Dr
Green River WY 82935

Call Sign: WA0ZWI
Bradley L Moe
610 Knotty Pine
Green River WY 82935

Call Sign: KC7YM
Dale E Johnson
1213 Log Cabin
Green River WY 82935

Call Sign: WB7DJ
Dale E Johnson
1213 Log Cabin
Green River WY 82935

Call Sign: KD7GHO
Doug Degase
2245 Maryland Ave
Green River WY 82935

Call Sign: KK7VD
Doug Degase
2245 Maryland Ave
Green River WY 82935

Call Sign: KC7IMF
Tim C Cassity
2265 Maryland Dr
Green River WY 82935

Call Sign: KC7CCI
David F Evans
63 N 5th W
Green River WY 82935

Call Sign: KC7CCH
Twyla M Evans
63 N 5th W
Green River WY 82935

Call Sign: WA7FKF
Alfred G Baker
190 N 6th W
Green River WY 82935

Call Sign: WB7QMO
Dallas K Bowen
2350 N Carolina Way
Green River WY 82935

Call Sign: KA7YRE
Scott T Polson
390 N Wagon Wheel Dr
Green River WY 82935

Call Sign: KB7LWU
Ivan B Banks
2105 New Hampshire
Green River WY 82935

Call Sign: KC7EYI
Richard W Hart
135 Powell St
Green River WY
829355021

Call Sign: N1TEK
Richard E Breininger
393 Ridge Crossing Unit B
Green River WY 82935

Call Sign: N7WYS
John P White
755 River View Dr 11
Green River WY 82935

Call Sign: N7COA
David L Gregory
1000 S Dakota
Green River WY 82935

Call Sign: KF7URT
Scott A Braithwaite
1370 Singletree Dr
Green River WY 82935

Call Sign: AA7WS
Gerry A Ferrin
472 Tollgate Ave
Green River WY 82935

Call Sign: KE7LUI
Phyllis J Dixon
523 Tollgate Ave
Green River WY 82935

Call Sign: KE7LVN
Richard W Dixon
523 Tollgate Ave
Green River WY 82935

Call Sign: KA7LWD
Francis J Fletcher
1055 Trona Dr

Green River WY 82935

Call Sign: K7LEB
Leonard E Bobbitt
1065 Trona Dr
Green River WY 82935

Call Sign: KE7KVQ
Leonard E Bobbitt
1065 Trona Dr
Green River WY 82935

Call Sign: KD7NWM
Christopher J Pritchard
1815 Virginia Dr
Green River WY 82935

Call Sign: N7IBM
Anthony J Coppola Jr
639 W 2nd North
Green River WY 82935

Call Sign: KF7SKW
Helen V Schalow
660 W 2nd North St
Green River WY 82935

Call Sign: WB7L
James H Probst
2360 W Teton
Green River WY 82935

Call Sign: KC8NIR
Kenneth W Birck
2045 W Teton Blvd
Green River WY 82935

Call Sign: KB7ZEF
Austin C Daniel
1585 Wyoming Dr
Green River WY 82935

Call Sign: KC7CCJ
Larry P Harjala
2230 Wyoming Dr

Green River WY 82935

Call Sign: N7QBW
Andrew L Parker
Green River WY 82935

Call Sign: N7QBT
Daryl A Parker
Green River WY 82935

Call Sign: KC7EDH
Dario Gonzalez Jr
Green River WY
829350821

Call Sign: WB7NKK
David F Hyer
Green River WY 82935

FCC Amateur Radio Licenses in Greybull

Call Sign: N7YGO
Michael L Scott
208 3rd Ave S
Greybull WY 82426

Call Sign: K6TN
Oral R Harvey Mr
233 5th Av N Unit 1
Greybull WY 82426

Call Sign: KC7EMU
Mark V Stamstad
Box 46
Greybull WY 82426

Call Sign: N7NNW
Douglas C Scott
216 Hilltop Dr
Greybull WY 82426

Call Sign: WY7DS
Douglas C Scott
216 Hilltop Dr

Greybull WY 82426

Call Sign: N4AHQ
Ernest L Smith
96 Hwy 20 S
Greybull WY 824269526

Call Sign: WB7TEZ
Tim R Sanderson
2360 US Hwy 20 W
Greybull WY 82426

Call Sign: WA7JHE
Bruce W Bergstrom
Greybull WY 82426

Call Sign: KB0CUC
Cynthia A Johnson
Greybull WY 82426

Call Sign: KD0T
Timothy D Johnson
Greybull WY 82426

FCC Amateur Radio Licenses in Grover

Call Sign: KD7GZG
Eric J Nelson
Grover WY 83122

FCC Amateur Radio Licenses in Guernsey

Call Sign: N8OUO
Carl G Be Vier
1036 Cottonwood Rd
Guernsey WY 82214

Call Sign: K7OUO
Carl G Be Vier
1036 Cottonwood Rd
Guernsey WY 82214

Call Sign: KD7OCG

Michelle E Schein
451 W Pittsburg St
Guernsey WY 82214

Call Sign: WW0K
Steve A Moyer
Guernsey WY 82214

Call Sign: KK7CN
Randolph J Schein
Guernsey WY 82214

Call Sign: KF7SAS
John E Offe
Guernsey WY 82214

Call Sign: KF7SAU
Thomas D Peterson
Guernsey WY 82214

FCC Amateur Radio Licenses in Hanna

Call Sign: KB7MRG
William J Waller
Hanna WY 82327

Call Sign: K7DU
George A Cummings
Hanna WY 823270657

Call Sign: KF7JPE
Peter S Lang
Hanna WY 82327

FCC Amateur Radio Licenses in Hillsdale

Call Sign: KD7YBL
Cara A Nelson
4231 Main
Hillsdale WY 82060

FCC Amateur Radio Licenses in Horse Creek

Call Sign: KE7FKP
Terry L Siegfried Jr
Horse Creek WY 82061

Call Sign: W7TLS
Terry L Siegfried Jr
Horse Creek WY 82061

FCC Amateur Radio Licenses in Hudson

Call Sign: KE7GDG
Ida E Hart
Hudson WY 82515

FCC Amateur Radio Licenses in Hulett

Call Sign: KC7FCS
Dan H Sachau
215 Birch
Hulett WY 82720

Call Sign: N7KXR
Irvin E Brimmer
Box 12
Hulett WY 82720

Call Sign: KC7OKC
James R Bush
447 Grazing Rd
Hulett WY 827209642

Call Sign: NZ7R
Elizabeth W Lyons
356 Holmes Rd
Hulett WY 82720

Call Sign: AC7LU
Charles B Scarborough
207 Missouri Butte Rd
Hulett WY 82720

Call Sign: KD7MLX

Sheila F Scarborough
207 Missouri Butte Rd
Hulett WY 82720

Call Sign: N7RBV
Wayne C Baker
Hulett WY 82720

FCC Amateur Radio Licenses in Jackson

Call Sign: KB7UZF
Kurt A Wimberg
2375 Apache Rd
Jackson WY 83001

Call Sign: WA7LOW
Corrie L Lovercheck
Box 1828
Jackson WY 83001

Call Sign: KB7UZK
Christopher Peck
Box 2548
Jackson WY 83001

Call Sign: WA4UMN
Brent A Blue
Box 3370
Jackson WY 83001

Call Sign: NW7D
Owen L Anderson
Box 392
Jackson WY 83001

Call Sign: KA0WYD
Sara L Sommers
Box 7235
Jackson WY 83002

Call Sign: KD7AWR
Weldon T Richardson Jr
247 E Broadway
Jackson WY 830011189

Call Sign: K6TJM
Thomas J Mccann Jr
525 E Golf Creek Ln 34
Jackson WY 83001

Call Sign: K7TJM
Thomas J Mccann Jr
525 E Golf Creek Ln 34
Jackson WY 83001

Call Sign: WB2TSV
Donald J Plumley
315 E Hansen St
Jackson WY 830012115

Call Sign: KF7CZD
Jane E Squires
400 E Sagebrush Dr
Jackson WY 83001

Call Sign: KF7UXY
James A Ligori
450 E Sagebrush Dr
Jackson WY 83001

Call Sign: KD7QAI
Ryan D Martell
5700 E Zenith Rd
Jackson WY 83001

Call Sign: K7EDA
Jeffrey P Mc Donald
1355 Hoyt Ln
Jackson WY 83001

Call Sign: KN6LL
John M Sherwood
235 N Cache St
Jackson WY 830011928

Call Sign: KF7IBQ
Tim A Jacobson
455 N Meadowlark Rd
Jackson WY 830019425

Call Sign: KF7IBS
Warren L Machol
500 N Westridge
Jackson WY 83001

Call Sign: WA7GHW
Mathew H Montagne
870 Ponderosa Dr
Jackson WY 83001

Call Sign: WB7CQS
James A Stone
65 Redmond St
Jackson WY 83001

Call Sign: KF7INK
Dee J Rammell
7700 S Hwy 89
Jackson WY 83001

Call Sign: KB4KVJ
Richard W Solon
6205 Spring Gulch Rd
Jackson WY 830011106

Call Sign: KE7THE
Frederick W Kortum
7705 Spring Gulch Rd
Jackson WY 83001

Call Sign: W7JVD
Fredrick W Kortum
7705 Spring Gulch Rd
Jackson WY 83001

Call Sign: WB7AXX
Stuart M Palmer
150 Sylvia Dr
Jackson WY 83001

Call Sign: KD7AWS
George L Thompson
808 Upper Redmond
Jackson WY 83001

Call Sign: KD7VFT
Gary L Isbell
970 W Broadway 322
Jackson WY 830027607

Call Sign: KC7PCD
Douglas G Mc Graw
785 W Sagebrush
Jackson WY 83001

Call Sign: K7JXN
Frank D Burchfield
Jackson WY 83001

Call Sign: KS7WY
Leroy M Dennis Jr
Jackson WY 830027685

Call Sign: K7JAC
Jackson Hole Area
Amateur Radio Club
Jackson WY 83002

Call Sign: AH3D
Martti J Laine
Jackson WY 83001

Call Sign: KC6KOU
Petri J Laine
Jackson WY 83001

Call Sign: KG7UC
Jeffrey P Mc Donald
Jackson WY 83001

Call Sign: KB7QKH
Katherine R Stone
Jackson WY 83001

Call Sign: KC7WQW
Matthew R Carlin
Jackson WY 83001

Call Sign: N3OID

David J Dean Sr
Jackson WY 83002

Call Sign: W7CAT
Michael L Dettmer
Jackson WY 83002

Call Sign: KC7FAL
Michael L Dettmer
Jackson WY 830017992

Call Sign: KE6XO
Charles E Donnelly
Jackson WY 83001

Call Sign: KE7UUW
Emergency
Communications Ham
Operators Jackson Hole
Jackson WY 83002

Call Sign: N7EJH
Emergency
Communications Ham
Operators Jackson Hole
Jackson WY 83002

Call Sign: KL1HF
Rebekah E Fors
Jackson WY 83002

Call Sign: KC7WWH
Cody M Hansen
Jackson WY 83002

Call Sign: KC7VXI
David B Macfarlane
Jackson WY 83001

Call Sign: N7DBM
David B Macfarlane
Jackson WY 83001

Call Sign: N7NG
Wayne A Mills

Jackson WY 83001

Call Sign: KD7BKR
Paul D Pearce
Jackson WY 83002

Call Sign: N7ZHP
Jim C Pigg Jr
Jackson WY 83002

Call Sign: KC7VPH
Michael D Reed
Jackson WY 83002

Call Sign: WA2TRF
David J Ryan
Jackson WY 83002

Call Sign: KC7FIL
Joshua R Schoeneberg
Jackson WY 83002

Call Sign: N7NHK
Scott A Stone
Jackson WY 83001

Call Sign: N1FPD
Fritz Szoncso
Jackson WY 83001

Call Sign: KE7CIN
Teton Amateur Radio
Repeater Association
Jackson WY 83002

Call Sign: W7TAR
Teton Amateur Radio
Repeater Association
Jackson WY 83002

Call Sign: KE7CXO
Teton Radio Amateur Club
Jackson WY 83002

Call Sign: WA7IFX

James Van Nostrand
Jackson WY 83001

Call Sign: KD7CAG
John G Woiwode
Jackson WY 83001

Call Sign: KD7HXI
David F Young
Jackson WY 83001

Call Sign: KF7QEY
Attila Sandor
Jackson WY 83002

Call Sign: WY7ET
Barry G Dyke
Jackson WY 83001

Call Sign: WY7JH
Barry G Dyke
Jackson WY 83001

Call Sign: KE7FIN
Ben M Ferrin
Jackson WY 83001

Call Sign: KF7IPC
Brian M Gardner
Jackson WY 83002

Call Sign: K7ZOO
Charles T Burd
Jackson WY 83001

Call Sign: KD7SJY
Charles T Burd
Jackson WY 83001

Call Sign: KD7YNG
Craig Harmening
Jackson WY 83001

Call Sign: KE7IAS
Craig W Flanick

Jackson WY 83002

Call Sign: K7JHL
David A Hodges
Jackson WY 83002

Call Sign: KF7IPB
David A Hodges
Jackson WY 83002

Call Sign: KD5USV
David B Abbey
Jackson WY 83002

Call Sign: KD7YNH
Elizabeth Harmening
Jackson WY 83001

Call Sign: K7FCH
Ferenc Csorja
Jackson WY 83002

Call Sign: KE7IRM
Ferenc Csorja
Jackson WY 83002

Call Sign: AD7FI
James D Waters
Jackson WY 83002

Call Sign: KE7AQJ
James D Waters
Jackson WY 83002

Call Sign: KE7MGT
Jeff S Miller
Jackson WY 83001

Call Sign: KE7GYA
John H Turi
Jackson WY 83002

Call Sign: KE7GXX
Kenneth A Stone
Jackson WY 830012346

Call Sign: KF7IOX
Kiley R Campbell
Jackson WY 83002

Call Sign: K7YJX
Krista L Nethercott
Jackson WY 83001

Call Sign: KF7IBP
Krista L Nethercott
Jackson WY 83001

Call Sign: KF7QEU
Kyle R Carmichael
Jackson WY 83002

Call Sign: KF7IOZ
Neal C Nethercott
Jackson WY 83001

Call Sign: KE7SDI
Peter C Ninnemann
Jackson WY 83001

Call Sign: KF7IGG
Richard A Palmer
Jackson WY 83001

Call Sign: KE7PRV
Richard R Ochs
Jackson WY 830023402

Call Sign: K7RLR
Rose L Robertson
Jackson WY 83001

Call Sign: KD7SJX
Rose L Robertson
Jackson WY 83001

Call Sign: KF7IOY
Russell H Ruschill
Jackson WY 83002

Call Sign: KF7IBR
Stacy R Kurtti
Jackson WY 83001

Call Sign: KE7SDJ
Thomas G Ninnemann
Jackson WY 83001

Call Sign: KE7NWG
Walter P Kirby
Jackson WY 83002

Call Sign: KD7SJZ
Wayne C Clayton
Jackson WY 83001

Call Sign: KE7LSH
William E Vogler
Jackson WY 83002

Call Sign: KE7GXY
Zachary C Rosser
Jackson WY 83001

FCC Amateur Radio Licenses in Jackson Hole

Call Sign: N7NLM
Timothy W Groenstein
Box 8520
Jackson Hole WY
830028520

FCC Amateur Radio Licenses in Jeffrey City

Call Sign: KC7BNB
Jesse L Shull
Box 6
Jeffrey City WY 82310

Call Sign: KB7FDD
Richard W Abington
116 Cottonwood Cir Box
656

Jeffrey City WY 82310

Call Sign: KA7AXE
Dennis E Green
10 Deer Rd
Jelm WY 820639200

Call Sign: AA7BP
Roy G Adair
299 St Hwy 10
Jelm WY 82063

Call Sign: KC7NJW
Chuck E Young
1002 3rd W
Kemmerer WY 83101

Call Sign: KF7JZD
Joshua S Hagler
1900 Berry Dr
Kemmerer WY 83101

Call Sign: KB7VXC
Trudy Barnes
Box 706
Kemmerer WY 83101

Call Sign: KC7HRT
Larry E Hultquist
1010 Cedar Ave
Kemmerer WY 83101

Call Sign: W7PIF
Clifford N Turner
1119 Cedar Ave
Kemmerer WY 83101

Call Sign: W7ERC
Veda C Turner

1119 Cedar Ave
Kemmerer WY 83101

Call Sign: KC7FHO
Harold L Wood
1430 Coulson Ave
Kemmerer WY 83101

Call Sign: KC7PRK
David L Spencer
905 Elk St
Kemmerer WY 83101

Call Sign: KC7MUY
Verlaine M Spencer
905 Elk St
Kemmerer WY 83101

Call Sign: KF7JZE
Vincent W Hinshaw
1121 Lupine Ln
Kemmerer WY 83101

Call Sign: KB7VXD
Angelene Barnes
1609 N Sunlight Dr
Kemmerer WY 83101

Call Sign: KA7YKU
David O Shubert
514 Onyx St
Kemmerer WY 83101

Call Sign: N7GJL
Gary J Leming
422 Sapphire St
Kemmerer WY 83101

Call Sign: KC7LNM
Lori A Bryson
1320 Sorensen Dr
Kemmerer WY 83101

Call Sign: KC7FDO
Lynn R Bryson

1320 Sorensen Dr
Kemmerer WY 83101

Call Sign: KF7EHE
Michael S Bryson
1320 Sorensen Dr
Kemmerer WY 83101

Call Sign: KF7EHD
Matthew S Bryson
1320 Sorensen Dr
Kemmerer WY 83101

Call Sign: KF7FTM
John L Smith
410 Willow Ave
Kemmerer WY 83101

Call Sign: N7UXF
Roger K Palmer
Kemmerer WY 83101

Call Sign: KB7FFN
Robert N Price
Kemmerer WY 83101

Call Sign: KC7HYB
Carolyn F Hultquist
Kemmerer WY 83101

Call Sign: N7UEL
Afton Robbins
Kemmerer WY 831011283

Call Sign: N7XHL
Roland L Robbins
Kemmerer WY 83101

Call Sign: KC7QXF
Zachary L Tyrrell
Kemmerer WY 83101

Call Sign: KB7ZEG
Linda C Wood
Kemmerer WY 831010842

Call Sign: KA7SHX
Robert S Wood
Kemmerer WY 83101

FCC Amateur Radio Licenses in Kinnear

Call Sign: KB0GQU
Arlene G Longie
11667 Hwy 26 Box 65
Kinnear WY 82516

Call Sign: KB0GQS
Joshua J Longie
11667 Hwy 26 Box 65
Kinnear WY 82516

Call Sign: W7LWR
Gerald A Yennie
11163 US Hwy 26
Kinnear WY 82516

Call Sign: N2NEP
John R Cunliffe
Kinnear WY 82516

Call Sign: NL7MW
Casimir T Gadomski
Kinnear WY 82516

FCC Amateur Radio Licenses in Kirby

Call Sign: AB7SQ
Daniel L Bare
221 W Main
Kirby WY 82430

FCC Amateur Radio Licenses in La Grange

Call Sign: KA7ZLL
Shirley K Sanders
Box 127

La Grange WY 82221

Call Sign: KC0JWA
Richard A Johnson
701 Hwy 151
La Grange WY 82221

Call Sign: N7KRU
Hazel M Sanders
4746 Hwy 151
La Grange WY 82221

Call Sign: WA7Q
Thomas L Sanders
4746 Hwy 151
La Grange WY 82221

Call Sign: KC0JWB
Carolyn S Johnson
701 Hyw 151
La Grange WY 82221

Call Sign: N7JPV
Frank T Sanders Jr
Route 79
La Grange WY 82221

Call Sign: KB7RQS
Francis W Hamilton
Rt 77
La Grange WY 82221

Call Sign: KC7HWS
Steven M Sanders
Rt 77 Box 271
La Grange WY 82221

FCC Amateur Radio Licenses in Lander

Call Sign: WA7OEC
Wilbert L Bregar
615 6th St Ct
Lander WY 82520

Call Sign: KE7FSM
Thomas N Dirks
245 Amoretti
Lander WY 82520

Call Sign: KE7VHA
Forrest G Phillips
445 And One Half N 8th St
Lander WY 82520

Call Sign: KB7JHQ
Dennis J Ashley
24 Birchfield Ln
Lander WY 82520

Call Sign: KF7KNI
Richard P Winslow
26 Bristlecone Rd
Lander WY 82520

Call Sign: K7TXZ
Edward A Erlandson
376 Cascade
Lander WY 82520

Call Sign: WB7SQV
Larry J King
594 Cross St
Lander WY 82520

Call Sign: K7LJK
Larry J King
594 Cross St
Lander WY 82520

Call Sign: KD7QDW
Frederick R Wendel
43 Deer Valley Dr
Lander WY 825209780

Call Sign: W7DRL
David R Langerman
120 Dupont Dr
Lander WY 82520

Call Sign: N7JYX
John R Mortensen
165 Dupont Dr
Lander WY 82520

Call Sign: KE7SXP
William T Acord
346 Market St
Lander WY 82520

Call Sign: KC7VXF
Eric R Jacobsen
30 Pheasant Run
Lander WY 82520

Call Sign: KB7UNT
Andrew C Hanson
1460 Goodrich Dr
Lander WY 82520

Call Sign: N7UQY
Ralph E Holcomb
1255 Mc Dougal Dr
Lander WY 82520

Call Sign: N7HYF
Eric B Struna
465 Popo Agie St
Lander WY 82520

Call Sign: KC7FAT
Glen P Revere
120 Indian Lookout Dr
Lander WY 82520

Call Sign: K4XE
James H Nelson
985 Mc Dougall Dr
Lander WY 82520

Call Sign: N7SVY
George F Gunsaullus
2 Russian Olive Ln
Lander WY 82520

Call Sign: KD7FZY
Coleen K Coleman
550 Jefferson St
Lander WY 825202126

Call Sign: KD7YJR
Richard S Hartman
1255 Mcdougal Dr
Lander WY 82520

Call Sign: K7RHA
Janay D Parent
101 S 2nd Apt 5
Lander WY 82520

Call Sign: N9JSL
Judith A Atnip
19 Juniper Dr
Lander WY 82520

Call Sign: W7VTB
Robert E Downs
2490 Mortimore Ln
Lander WY 82520

Call Sign: KC7RHA
Janay D Parent
101 S 2nd Apt 5
Lander WY 82520

Call Sign: KD7OAS
Joshua M Murchison
345 Main St 19
Lander WY 82520

Call Sign: KC7FAU
David P Revere
220 Mt Arter Loop
Lander WY 825202920

Call Sign: KD7AJZ
Bobby L Johnston
325 S 7th
Lander WY 82520

Call Sign: KE7JZR
Owen O Pitt
478 Market
Lander WY 82520

Call Sign: WA7RGO
Robert L Millis
640 N 10th St
Lander WY 82520

Call Sign: WA0TUT
Patrick M Lindsay
151 S 9th St
Lander WY 82520

Call Sign: W7OOP
Owen O Pitt
478 Market
Lander WY 82520

Call Sign: WB7AHL
Bobby L Johnston
493 N 2nd
Lander WY 82520

Call Sign: KD7DTV
Tara L Stueckler
36 Shadowbrook Ln
Lander WY 82520

Call Sign: KD7PQG
Kenneth J Martin
607 Market 4
Lander WY 82520

Call Sign: WB7AHL
Donald R Johnston
493 N 2nd St
Lander WY 82520

Call Sign: NL7TD
J Daniel Roach
580 Tweed Ln
Lander WY 82520

Call Sign: N7UPG
David R Kallgren
877 V1 Rd
Lander WY 82520

Call Sign: KB9YWN
Dominick J Weigel Jr.
778 Victory Ln
Lander WY 82520

Call Sign: WB7CJT
Gary F Gordon
157 Wood St
Lander WY 82520

Call Sign: KD7PPP
Fremont County Amateur
Radio Society
300 Wood St
Lander WY 82520

Call Sign: KC7GAQ
Raymond H Snyder
300 Wood St
Lander WY 82520

Call Sign: WJ7V
Raymond H Snyder
300 Wood St
Lander WY 82520

Call Sign: KB7UZC
Brent G Bills
Lander WY 82520

Call Sign: KB7YCE
Jennifer Bills
Lander WY 82520

Call Sign: KB7UZD
Laural A Bills
Lander WY 82520

Call Sign: KB7WXN
Sarah A Bills

Lander WY 82520

Call Sign: KB5CAR
Buddy W Green
Lander WY 82520

Call Sign: KB7QPW
Peter W Kallgren
Lander WY 82520

Call Sign: N7UPD
Leslie F Van Barselaar
Lander WY 82520

Call Sign: KE7PEQ
Terri L Watson
Lander WY 82520

**FCC Amateur Radio
Licenses in Laramie**

Call Sign: AD7UB
Douglas C Frick
1071 Alta Vista Dr
Laramie WY 82072

Call Sign: KE7TJB
Douglas C Frick
1071 Alta Vista Dr
Laramie WY 82072

Call Sign: KE7TWS
Marie D Frick
1071 Alta Vista Dr
Laramie WY 82072

Call Sign: N7NTG
Jeffrey C Van Slyke
1413 Baker St
Laramie WY 82070

Call Sign: KB7VDM
James J Waldram
1508 Beaufort St
Laramie WY 82070

Call Sign: KB6DRM
James C Schatzman
1619 Beaufort St
Laramie WY 82071

Call Sign: KF7UZC
Gerald J Bucher
1408 Beaufort St
Laramie WY 82072

Call Sign: KD7W
William D Wheeler
1810 Bill Nye Ave
Laramie WY 82070

Call Sign: KD7GDB
Donna J Kunselman
16 Black Elk Trl
Laramie WY 82070

Call Sign: KD7GDC
Raymond Kunselman
16 Black Elk Trl
Laramie WY 820705354

Call Sign: KD7GWV
Raymond Kunselman
10 Black Elk Trl
Laramie WY 820705354

Call Sign: KD7HAG
Donna J Kunselman
16 Black Elk Trl
Laramie WY 820705354

Call Sign: KD7HNL
Donna J Kunselman
16 Black Elk Trl
Laramie WY 820705354

Call Sign: KD7HNK
Raymond Kunselman
16 Black Elk Trl
Laramie WY 820705354

Call Sign: AC7IN
Raymond Kunsglman
16 Black Elk Trl
Laramie WY 820705354

Call Sign: K7UMH
Dennis F Moore
1316 Canby St
Laramie WY 82070

Call Sign: NQ7Q
Wayne M Sutherland
28 Coyote St
Laramie WY 82072

Call Sign: KK7BR
Frank L Peters
150 Blackfoot St Unit 11
Laramie WY 820708323

Call Sign: KA7DHE
Allen W Tanner
4206 Cheyenne Dr
Laramie WY 82070

Call Sign: KE7AZJ
Jesse W Sutherland
28 Coyote St
Laramie WY 82072

Call Sign: WB7K
Francis R Mc Donald
4511 Bluebird Ln
Laramie WY 82070

Call Sign: KC7QCQ
Robert L Wolverton
4218 Cheyenne Dr
Laramie WY 82070

Call Sign: KC7JFV
Bishwa Shrestha
Crane Hall 313
Laramie WY 82070

Call Sign: KF7URO
Michael R Stephens
1722 Boswell Dr
Laramie WY 82070

Call Sign: AB7RH
Charles F Blake
209 Colorado Ave
Laramie WY 82070

Call Sign: N7KXP
Charlotte M James
4411 Crow D
Laramie WY 82070

Call Sign: N7YMQ
Alice M Sander
Box 1364
Laramie WY 82070

Call Sign: WY7O
Raymond Kunselman
4205 Comanche Dr
Laramie WY 82072

Call Sign: N7KXO
James M James
4411 Crow D
Laramie WY 82070

Call Sign: N7XNJ
Frank J Sander
Box 1364
Laramie WY 82070

Call Sign: KD7RQX
Doris L Hutcheson
4431 Comanche Dr
Laramie WY 82072

Call Sign: KF7UZQ
Bradley B Thomas
2667 Dadisman St
Laramie WY 82070

Call Sign: KB7SFL
Bruce B Mitchell
Box 758
Laramie WY 82070

Call Sign: KD7NAE
John M Harrison
4431 Comanche Dr
Laramie WY 82072

Call Sign: W7EAF
Leslie H Klahn
2813 Dover Dr
Laramie WY 82072

Call Sign: WB7DDT
Roy E Davis
607 Bradley
Laramie WY 82070

Call Sign: WB3BD
Gerard P Andrews
216 Corthell Rd
Laramie WY 82070

Call Sign: KD7LTI
David E Cook
710 Downey St 11
Laramie WY 82072

Call Sign: KB7WOK
Jana M Howard
802 Bradley St
Laramie WY 82070

Call Sign: K7JMS
Judy M Sutherland
28 Coyote St
Laramie WY 82070

Call Sign: KK7VY
Scott C Carlson
1302 E Canby St
Laramie WY 82072

Call Sign: KB7Z
Michael C Humphreys
911 E Curtis St
Laramie WY 82072

Call Sign: WB5YWQ
John G Williams
1312 E Park
Laramie WY 820704146

Call Sign: WB0YZN
David K Yeutter
6 French Creek Rd
Laramie WY 82070

Call Sign: KF7AQV
Alexandra F Schlump
1005 E Custer St
Laramie WY 82070

Call Sign: KC7QDF
Martha S Williams
1312 E Park Ave
Laramie WY 82070

Call Sign: WB0YZM
Marilyn K Yeutter
6 French Creek Rd
Laramie WY 82070

Call Sign: N7JT
Jerry D Tastad
519 E Flint St
Laramie WY 82070

Call Sign: W7JAL
John F Mc Kay
2461 E Park Ave
Laramie WY 82070

Call Sign: W7STD
Scott T Dean
3325 Ft Sanders Rd 23
Laramie WY 82070

Call Sign: KB7SGP
Lynn E Hamblin
1947 E Garfield
Laramie WY 82070

Call Sign: KE6ZBM
Robert B Dryer
2207 E Sheridan
Laramie WY 82070

Call Sign: KB7SGR
James L Petty
1706 Garfield
Laramie WY 82070

Call Sign: KD7IFH
Matthew J Hornbach
1414 E Gibbon St Apt A3
Laramie WY 82072

Call Sign: KE7MXO
John W Pearce
4746 E Skyline 46
Laramie WY 82070

Call Sign: K7CMJ
Andrew H Lessenden
1907 Garfield
Laramie WY 82070

Call Sign: KF7OEM
Brett D Miller
1500 E Grand Ave
Laramie WY 82070

Call Sign: KD7FHE
Richard W Jones
4746 E Skyline Dr 55
Laramie WY 82070

Call Sign: KC7GGI
Dylan M Littlefield
1007 Gibbon 2
Laramie WY 82070

Call Sign: KB7VQV
Barry A Mather
1419 E Kearney St
Laramie WY 82070

Call Sign: KC7OJX
Nicholas R Hardgrove
1209 Flint 2
Laramie WY 82070

Call Sign: N7KXQ
Jason A Gonzales
1426 Grafton St
Laramie WY 82072

Call Sign: KE7APN
Michael N Thatcher
508 E Lyon St Apt 3
Laramie WY 82072

Call Sign: KC7AXI
Eric J Tastad
519 Flint St
Laramie WY 82070

Call Sign: KA7GAA
Victor A Ryan
1202 Grand Ave E
Laramie WY 82070

Call Sign: K0SDT
Shane D Toven
1123 E Palmer Dr
Laramie WY 82070

Call Sign: WB7VTT
Jack R Dempsey
4326 Foothills St
Laramie WY 82070

Call Sign: N7VOM
Robert A Middleton
1154 Granito Dr
Laramie WY 820705027

Call Sign: KA7WTR
David L Silvey
1006 Harney
Laramie WY 82070

Call Sign: N7KCZ
Jerry D Boling
236 Lewis Rd
Laramie WY 82070

Call Sign: KC7QHY
Gary C Wilkerson
5410 Meadow Ln
Laramie WY 820205725

Call Sign: WA7NOI
George A Twitchell
786 Hwy 230
Laramie WY 82070

Call Sign: KF7TRQ
Corin D Chepko
718 Lewis St Apt A
Laramie WY 82072

Call Sign: KC7QCP
Norma N Wilkerson
5410 Meadow Ln
Laramie WY 820705725

Call Sign: K7NOI
George A Twitchell
786 Hwy 230
Laramie WY 82070

Call Sign: KA7YJN
Keith M Aurzada
2627 Lodgepole Ln 625
Laramie WY 82070

Call Sign: N7VON
Linda G Martin
4605 Meadowlark
Laramie WY 82073

Call Sign: KB7GSJ
Matthew P Magee
1171 Inca Dr
Laramie WY 82070

Call Sign: KC7HNM
Chris O Bonser
708 Lyons
Laramie WY 82070

Call Sign: N7SVJ
Robert H Sutherland
4605 Meadowlark Ln
Laramie WY 82070

Call Sign: KC7WXW
Dennis A Mundt
1585 Inca Dr
Laramie WY 82072

Call Sign: W7LE
John F Escobedo
954 Mc Cue 43
Laramie WY 82070

Call Sign: KD7RJP
Louis W Sims
1326 Mill St
Laramie WY 82072

Call Sign: KF7KEY
Carrie A Ferguson
17 Jack Rabbit Rd
Laramie WY 82070

Call Sign: KD7AJS
Rebecca S Gonzales
954 Mc Cue St 23
Laramie WY 82072

Call Sign: AE7HH
Louis W Sims
1326 Mill St
Laramie WY 82072

Call Sign: KD7BOU
Craig A Hutcheson
529 Johnson St
Laramie WY 82070

Call Sign: KB7USL
Yasuhiro Ota
228 Mc Intyre Hall
Laramie WY 82070

Call Sign: WY7LS
Louis W Sims
1326 Mill St
Laramie WY 82072

Call Sign: KD7KMT
Laura J Harris
4120 Kiowa Dr
Laramie WY 82072

Call Sign: W7EMA
Ora L Newberry Jr
954 Mccue Lot 119
Laramie WY 82072

Call Sign: K7ANW
Scott B Smithson
61 Millbrook Rd
Laramie WY 820709727

Call Sign: W9TWR
Jerry T Boling
245 Lewis Rd
Laramie WY 82070

Call Sign: KD7KMU
James A Johnson
5203 Meadow Ln
Laramie WY 82070

Call Sign: N7SXC
William H Frazier
804 Mitchell
Laramie WY 82072

Call Sign: KD7NEZ
Dale W Dilworth
1126 Mitchell St
Laramie WY 82072

Call Sign: N7KPI
Gregory T Kent
2071 N 15th St
Laramie WY 82070

Call Sign: N7OQZ
Christine F Woods
265 N 7th Apt 144
Laramie WY 82070

Call Sign: N3KBP
Dale W Dilworth
1126 Mitchell St
Laramie WY 82072

Call Sign: KE7MXP
Robert G Roe
2267 N 15th St
Laramie WY 820721805

Call Sign: KB7SGQ
Scott M Tisinger
1260 N 7th St
Laramie WY 82070

Call Sign: KD7KGB
Glenn A Carlson
1215 Mitchell St
Laramie WY 82072

Call Sign: KD7LDA
Kimberly M Carlson
1461 N 17th St
Laramie WY 82072

Call Sign: KC7ZRS
Justin W Johnson
664 N 8th
Laramie WY 82072

Call Sign: WB7CPP
Edith W Hirsch
11 Mountain Meadow Rd
Laramie WY 82070

Call Sign: KS7Q
Fred B Crowell
2166 N 17th St
Laramie WY 82072

Call Sign: KF7EBL
Roberta J Johnson
664 N 8th St
Laramie WY 82072

Call Sign: WB7BKM
Fred H Hirsch
11 Mountain Meadow Rd
Laramie WY 82070

Call Sign: WB7I
Holly Crowell
2166 N 17th St
Laramie WY 82072

Call Sign: KB7GUE
David E Steidtmann
953 N 9th
Laramie WY 82070

Call Sign: KX7S
Henry L Schroeder
663 N 10th St
Laramie WY 82070

Call Sign: KD7TVU
Chad S Mitchell
1171 N 17th St C
Laramie WY 82072

Call Sign: KU7D
Millard C Johnson
566 N 9th St
Laramie WY 82070

Call Sign: KF7UZE
Jeffrey A Parkins
466 N 11th St Apt A
Laramie WY 82072

Call Sign: KA7GPF
Andrew A Aronson
671 N 4th St
Laramie WY 82070

Call Sign: KY0DR
David A Rush
261 N Cedar St
Laramie WY 820723503

Call Sign: KC7DPR
Jack Harrop
967 N 12
Laramie WY 82070

Call Sign: KD7DYO
Richard N Jones
754 N 5th St
Laramie WY 82072

Call Sign: KC5BLT
Keith W Schmauss
1664 N Cedar St Lot 16
Laramie WY 820726738

Call Sign: AF7E
William H Wright
1856 N 13th St
Laramie WY 820721934

Call Sign: KA0AKZ
Adell D Higgins
2052 N 7th 16
Laramie WY 82070

Call Sign: KA7VMA
Dick L Wynes
282 N Fillmore
Laramie WY 82070

Call Sign: KJ7IM
Rhett A Downing
954 N Mc Cue 159
Laramie WY 82070

Call Sign: N0FT
Lafonne J Taylor
866 N Pine St
Laramie WY 82072

Call Sign: KB7SFM
Doris R Van Slyke
262 N Taylor 27
Laramie WY 82070

Call Sign: WB7BUP
James R Kirkpatrick
4212 Navajo Dr
Laramie WY 82070

Call Sign: WA7LEK
Maryanne M Kirkpatrick
4212 Navajo Dr
Laramie WY 82072

Call Sign: KB7NCH
A Scott Corcoran
2521 Overland Rd
Laramie WY 82070

Call Sign: KC7WWE
Sylvia A Hansen
1213 Palmer Dr
Laramie WY 820704645

Call Sign: KB7USJ
Joe B Teeter
1216 Palmer Dr
Laramie WY 82070

Call Sign: N7QIZ
Charles C Nash
1807 Park Ave
Laramie WY 82070

Call Sign: KB7CSD
Gilbert J Batz
1521 Person St
Laramie WY 82070

Call Sign: AC7FJ
Anthony E Arnerich
2124 Rainbow Ave
Laramie WY 82070

Call Sign: KD7CEJ
Anthony E Arnerich
2124 Rainbow Ave
Laramie WY 82070

Call Sign: KB7QOM
Merl F Raisbeck
2852 Riverside
Laramie WY 82070

Call Sign: KC7DPQ
Marie A Fletcher
1581 Riverside Dr
Laramie WY 82070

Call Sign: WB7CJO
Walter R Fletcher
1581 Riverside Dr
Laramie WY 82070

Call Sign: KD7KGC
Denis M Walsh
2583 Riverside Dr
Laramie WY 82070

Call Sign: KE7DWD
Trevor M Walsh
2583 Riverside Dr
Laramie WY 82070

Call Sign: KB7ROH
Michael J Palmer
715 S 11th St
Laramie WY 82070

Call Sign: AC7SZ
Suzanne C Luhr
603 S 12th St
Laramie WY 82070

Call Sign: KD7NAF
Suzanne C Luhr
603 S 12th St
Laramie WY 82070

Call Sign: KD7PXK
Wes L Luhr
603 S 12th St
Laramie WY 82070

Call Sign: AA7AY
Suzanne C Luhr
603 S 12th St
Laramie WY 82070

Call Sign: KF7UFF
Benjamin R Morgan
401 S 15th St
Laramie WY 82070

Call Sign: KF7UFG
Corbin Haugen
401 S 15th St
Laramie WY 82070

Call Sign: KC7PBB
Donald L Shaner
716 S 22nd
Laramie WY 820704813

Call Sign: N7DLS
Donald L Shaner
716 S 22nd
Laramie WY 820704813

Call Sign: N7OSD
David B Lange
607 S 25th St
Laramie WY 82070

Call Sign: KF7UZF
Michael D Sullivan
407 S 25th St
Laramie WY 82070

Call Sign: KC7UGD
Ora L Newberry Jr
215 S 3rd 310
Laramie WY 820703621

Call Sign: KD7RMI
Michael D Wilson
620 S 6th St
Laramie WY 82070

Call Sign: KF7CJZ
Jake J Riske
107 S Adams
Laramie WY 82070

Call Sign: KC7WWD
Rhonda S John
702 S Eighth
Laramie WY 82070

Call Sign: KD7KXG
Kenneth P Kennedy
520 S Grant St
Laramie WY 82070

Call Sign: N7SPH
James R Ackerson
163 S Kiowa
Laramie WY 82070

Call Sign: KC7AXJ
Robert L Sutherland
1420 Sanders
Laramie WY 82070

Call Sign: KC7ZRR
Jane R Gonzales
105 Satanka Rd
Laramie WY 82070

Call Sign: N7OBS
Robert L Gonzales
105 Satanka Rd
Laramie WY 82070

Call Sign: KE7YUN
Jerrod R Gonzales
105 Satanka Rd
Laramie WY 82070

Call Sign: KA7HEJ
Ruth O Wright
1304 Sheridan
Laramie WY 82070

Call Sign: KB7BYO
Rose M Hughes
512 Sheridan St
Laramie WY 82070

Call Sign: KD7OMK
Myron B Allen III
1108 Sheridan St
Laramie WY 82070

Call Sign: W3MBA
Myron B Allen III
1108 Sheridan St
Laramie WY 82070

Call Sign: W7MO
Paul W Pheneger Jr
2310 Skyview Ln
Laramie WY 82070

Call Sign: N7UW
University Amateur Radio
Club
2310 Skyview Ln
Laramie WY 82070

Call Sign: K7OAE
Dean C Shaw
2092 State Hwy 230

Laramie WY 82070

Call Sign: KE7HTD
Gery D Simpson
404 Sth 30th 116
Laramie WY 82070

Call Sign: KD7ZHN
Johnnie R Scott Jr
Sunrise Ct
Laramie WY 82070

Call Sign: KD7CTP
Jerry C Hamann
1722 Symons
Laramie WY 820705451

Call Sign: N7OFI
Mark L Price
1932 Thornburgh
Laramie WY 82070

Call Sign: KK7AG
Ty R Bonser
2135 Thornburgh
Laramie WY 82070

Call Sign: KC7UGF
Gary Y York
26 Trotter Ln
Laramie WY 82070

Call Sign: KL0TF
Lessley B Coulthard
1564 Van Buren 2
Laramie WY 82070

Call Sign: KC7YFI
Jacob F Whiting
363 W Garfield Apt 4
Laramie WY 82072

Call Sign: N7CII
Robert F Kubichek
1601 W Hill Rd

Laramie WY 82072

Call Sign: KC7ZRT
Sharon L Kubichek
1601 W Hill Rd
Laramie WY 82072

Call Sign: KD7FHC
Shawn T Kubichek
1601 W Hill Rd
Laramie WY 82072

Call Sign: KB7FIB
David H Lew
1602 W Hill Rd
Laramie WY 82070

Call Sign: KF7UZO
Luke P Wood
1272 W Lyons St 45
Laramie WY 82072

Call Sign: KF7UZP
Misty R Wood
1272 W Lyons St 45
Laramie WY 82072

Call Sign: KD7IRF
Lyndall R Riedel
2673 W Nelson
Laramie WY 82070

Call Sign: N7QJL
Deborah E Welke
1875 W Snowy Range Rd
Laramie WY 82070

Call Sign: KD7KMS
James Hereford
365 W University Ave
Laramie WY 82072

Call Sign: N0PSC
Cameron H G Wright
35 Walgren Ln

Laramie WY 82070

Call Sign: KE7SZI
Robert A Grogan
White Hall
Laramie WY 82070

Call Sign: KF7DFU
Thomas K Brown
1514 Whitman
Laramie WY 82070

Call Sign: KB7KYL
Eugene D Duda
Laramie WY 82070

Call Sign: KB7JKH
Timothy E Kuhlman
Laramie WY 82070

Call Sign: WB7SUG
E Luella Magrath
Laramie WY 820731668

Call Sign: WB7RSB
Francis E Magrath
Laramie WY 820731668

Call Sign: KA7MPB
Dolores M Marshall
Laramie WY 82070

Call Sign: W7SE
Walter C Marshall
Laramie WY 82070

Call Sign: KB7SFK
Betty J Mitchell
Laramie WY 82070

Call Sign: N5CUT
Carl S Nordblom
Laramie WY 82070

Call Sign: KA7KGT

Robert L Sutherland
Laramie WY 82070

Call Sign: KB7UGN
Roger L Wilson
Laramie WY 82071

Call Sign: KA7QGP
Henry L Carpenter
Laramie WY 820730501

Call Sign: WL7CMA
Steve M Coulthard
Laramie WY 82073

Call Sign: N6NVF
Larry O Dean
Laramie WY 82071

Call Sign: AB1HZ
Former Operators Of
Hz1Ab
Laramie WY 82070

Call Sign: KC7IL
Stephen J Goldman
Laramie WY 820730238

Call Sign: KN6AL
Carl P Gottsmann
Laramie WY 820713531

Call Sign: N7GUD
Stephen J Grabowski
Laramie WY 82070

Call Sign: WA7SVH
Lloyd K Hashimoto
Laramie WY 82070

Call Sign: WA7LEA
Ronald W Marchitelli
Laramie WY 820730731

Call Sign: KD7FHF

John B Mc Donald
Laramie WY 820731142

Call Sign: KC7UGH
Leila Rita Stanfield
Laramie WY 82073

Call Sign: KC7QHX
John G Sutherland
Laramie WY 82070

Call Sign: KC6WZP
David M Young
Laramie WY 820731683

Call Sign: KF7UZD
Ellie A Riske
Laramie WY 82073

Call Sign: K7SIG
Jake J Riske
Laramie WY 820730505

Call Sign: KE7APO
Nancy L Sutherland
Laramie WY 82073

Call Sign: KF7UZB
Susan Hanna
Laramie WY 82073

FCC Amateur Radio Licenses in Lingle

Call Sign: KB7SX
Robert D Dorn
8481 Rd 39
Lingle WY 82223

Call Sign: N7MNW
Robert L Gorr Jr
Rt 1
Lingle WY 82223

Call Sign: N7LTC

Dori L Gorr
Rt 1
Lingle WY 82223

FCC Amateur Radio Licenses in Lovell

Call Sign: KB7USK
Alan L Pomeroy
258 Carmon Avenue
Lovell WY 82431

Call Sign: KA7MVY
Jerry F Wellman
855 Jersey Ave
Lovell WY 82431

Call Sign: KA7MVX
Patricia R Wellman
855 Jersey Ave
Lovell WY 82431

Call Sign: W7CA
John F Hall
1038 Lane 12
Lovell WY 82431

Call Sign: KC7EOU
Richard J Klundt
340 N Hwy 32
Lovell WY 82431

Call Sign: KC7NVI
Gary R Lentz
56 Oregon Av
Lovell WY 82431

FCC Amateur Radio Licenses in Lusk

Call Sign: N7HCR
Larry E La Maack
509 E 8th St
Lusk WY 82225

Call Sign: N7BDK
Quentin C Roberts
518 S Maple
Lusk WY 82225

Call Sign: N7YDH
Jerry S Schutt
205 W 7th
Lusk WY 82225

Call Sign: N7QLF
Jerry P Green
Lusk WY 82225

Call Sign: KK7LI
Dennis R Green
Lusk WY 82225

Call Sign: KE7ADS
Dirk B Joss
Lusk WY 82225

FCC Amateur Radio Licenses in Lyman

Call Sign: AE7FA
David E Olsen
301 First St
Lyman WY 82937

Call Sign: KC7OZQ
Phil J Koeven
110 Platts St
Lyman WY 82937

Call Sign: KF4LAR
Garlie C Davis Jr
127 W Owen
Lyman WY 82937

Call Sign: NS7R
Paul V Mac Donald
Lyman WY 82937

Call Sign: KF7USA

Bridger Valley Amateur
Radio Club
Lyman WY 82937

Call Sign: WY7BV
Bridger Valley Amateur
Radio Club
Lyman WY 82937

Call Sign: KG6LNC
David E Olsen
Lyman WY 82937

Call Sign: KC7ISD
Benjamin M Scofield
Lyman WY 82937

Call Sign: WB0GEH
Patrick D Smith
Lyman WY 82937

Call Sign: KF7OOD
Alan S Hinman
Lyman WY 82937

Call Sign: KF7RVN
Jeremiah L Jackson
Lyman WY 82937

Call Sign: KF7HOB
Patty A Olsen
Lyman WY 82937

FCC Amateur Radio Licenses in Mammoth Hot Springs

Call Sign: KC7ZYE
William G Hansen
Mammoth Hot Springs
WY 82190

FCC Amateur Radio Licenses in Manderson

Call Sign: KA7LNV
Beverly A Bennett
620 N Sherman Box 14
Manderson WY 82432

FCC Amateur Radio Licenses in Meeteetse

Call Sign: KB7VJM
Rulane B Merz
73 Black Diamond Dr
Meeteetse WY 82433

Call Sign: KC7GKJ
Travis J Richardson
18 Saddle Hill Rd
Meeteetse WY 82433

Call Sign: KC7MOA
Doty M Colling
Meeteetse WY 82433

Call Sign: KE7NPD
Alexander A Offley
Meeteetse WY 82433

Call Sign: KF7UIK
Edgar L Rapp
Meeteetse WY 82433

Call Sign: KE7RFL
James L Guelde
Meeteetse WY 824330276

FCC Amateur Radio Licenses in Mills

Call Sign: W7GRL
Gary R Lentz
201 Benton Ave
Mills WY 826440106

Call Sign: AE7LS
Gary R Lentz
201 Benton Ave

Mills WY 826440106

Call Sign: KC7ATW
Patrick N Kennedy
505 Benton St
Mills WY 82644

Call Sign: KB7UHN
William E Brite
Mills WY 82644

Call Sign: N7VLL
Richard D Doyle
Mills WY 82644

Call Sign: KB7GAB
Bernard R Laur
Mills WY 82644

Call Sign: K7VAD
Jeff Severn
Mills WY 826440605

Call Sign: W7BIG
Richard D Doyle
Mills WY 82644

Call Sign: WA4TWI
Alexander J Folts Jr
Mills WY 82644

Call Sign: KC7DHA
Jack D Francis
Mills WY 82644

Call Sign: KD7OAV
Thomas O Riegert
Mills WY 82649

Call Sign: KD7ASO
James E Samet
Mills WY 82644

Call Sign: W7ASO
James E Samet

Mills WY 82644

Call Sign: KC7WZW
Ken E Spriggs Jr.
Mills WY 82644

Call Sign: KC7WZV
Susan E Spriggs
Mills WY 82644

Call Sign: KF7OPT
Andrea U Lentz
Mills WY 82644

FCC Amateur Radio Licenses in Moorcroft

Call Sign: KD7IYW
Douglas J Kallemeyn
34 Pine Ridge Rd
Moorcroft WY 82721

Call Sign: KD7HXH
Kitty L Yelland
34 Pine Ridge Rd
Moorcroft WY 82721

Call Sign: N7HHJ
Jack R Welch
412 Sisson Ave
Moorcroft WY 82721

Call Sign: KD7KNZ
Wade J Dennis
Moorcroft WY 82721

Call Sign: KD7RDF
Jeff A Sipe
Moorcroft WY 82721

Call Sign: KE7LLM
Edmund L Ogle
Moorcroft WY 82721

Call Sign: KE7QVP

William J Sommer
Moorcroft WY 82721

FCC Amateur Radio Licenses in Moose

Call Sign: W7SLM
John F Turner
Triangle X Ranch
Moose WY 83012

Call Sign: KD7QWN
Ann E Blakley
Moose WY 83012

Call Sign: KD7OHN
John S Blakley
Moose WY 83012

Call Sign: KD7MQY
James F Cramer
Moose WY 83012

Call Sign: K7BAR
Marilyn V Jablonski
Moose WY 83012

Call Sign: KD7QWM
Marilyn V Jablonski
Moose WY 83012

Call Sign: KD7OPC
Duran S Saavedra
Moose WY 83012

Call Sign: W7AJK
Duran S Saavedra
Moose WY 83012

Call Sign: KF7QEX
Shawn C Lowery
Moose WY 83012

FCC Amateur Radio Licenses in Moran

Call Sign: NE9Z
William G Rinker
22450 E River Rock Rd
Moran WY 83013

Call Sign: WA7AUV
Lewis P Price Jr
Mtn View Ranch Box 248
Moran WY 83013

Call Sign: KJ4PSG
James V Warren Jr
PO Box 348
Moran WY 83013

Call Sign: KJ7WTF
James V Warren Jr
PO Box 348
Moran WY 83013

Call Sign: KF7CZE
Jon M White
Moran WY 83013

FCC Amateur Radio Licenses in Mountain View

Call Sign: KC7HBV
Thomas R Brailsford
215 6th St
Mountain View WY
829390988

Call Sign: K7GB
George A Baer
PO Box 546
Mountain View WY 82939

Call Sign: KC7DIX
John A Metcalfe
Mountain View WY 82939

Call Sign: KF7OOE

Dean M Podzamsky
Mountain View WY 82939

Call Sign: KF7RVK
Isaac D Lord
Mountain View WY 82939

Call Sign: KE7NIH
Jerry L Gunter
Mountain View WY 82939

FCC Amateur Radio Licenses in Newcastle

Call Sign: KD7ZUP
James D Kinney
211 6th Ave
Newcastle WY 82701

Call Sign: KC7EOF
James D Thorson
Box 338
Newcastle WY 82701

Call Sign: WB7QPA
Cyrus P Dopp
Box 39
Newcastle WY 82701

Call Sign: KD7RDB
Clarence L Baker
217 Frontier Ave
Newcastle WY 82701

Call Sign: KG7FI
Wayne B Erickson
130 S Seneca
Newcastle WY 82701

Call Sign: AB5SW
Johnny D Buehler Jr
3249 Section Line Rd
Newcastle WY 82701

Call Sign: KC5FHW

Linda M Buehler
3249 Section Line Rd
Newcastle WY 82701

Call Sign: KC7HWB
Charles R Meyer
15 Skyview Dr
Newcastle WY 82701

Call Sign: KF7QYA
Conrad J Farnsworth
23315 US Hwy 85 N
Newcastle WY 82701

Call Sign: W7ETR
Thomas D Wing
14 Wapiti Trl
Newcastle WY 82701

Call Sign: KD7QDM
Richard D Klinker
Newcastle WY 827010969

Call Sign: KD7ZIZ
Northeastern Wyo.
Amateur Radio Club
Newcastle WY 82701

Call Sign: KD7UOV
Brian E Klinker
Newcastle WY 82701

Call Sign: KE7ADR
Sherry A Wilson
Newcastle WY 82701

FCC Amateur Radio Licenses in Opal

Call Sign: KF7FTL
Donald P Hutchinson
Opal WY 83124

FCC Amateur Radio Licenses in Osage

Call Sign: KD7RDE
Nancy L Bock
Osage WY 827230321

FCC Amateur Radio Licenses in Parkman

Call Sign: KC7PXB
John R Johnston
691 Pass Creek Rd
Parkman WY 82838

Call Sign: KF7RUD
Robert J Schluter
Parkman WY 82838

FCC Amateur Radio Licenses in Pavillion

Call Sign: KE7KBE
Delmer L Howery Sr
104 E Washington
Pavillion WY 82523

Call Sign: KA0ODL
Edgar A L Allison
2280 Missouri Valley Rd
Pavillion WY 82523

Call Sign: KD7BBT
Marvin H Jordan Jr
113 Williams
Pavillion WY 82523

Call Sign: KB7FGN
Paul K Mc Tee
Pavillion WY 82523

Call Sign: KF7BJM
Emily A Howery
Pavillion WY 82523

FCC Amateur Radio Licenses in Pine Bluffs

Call Sign: KF7FAE
Donald N Wills
105 CR 161
Pine Bluffs WY 82082

Call Sign: KF7CJB
Craig L Herd
795 CR 161
Pine Bluffs WY 82082

Call Sign: KE7WMJ
Mark R Claeys Sr
6110 CR 210
Pine Bluffs WY 82082

Call Sign: WY7ML
Christine M Bingham
28 Buck Dr
Pine Haven WY 82721

Call Sign: WY7LL
Leo C Bingham
28 Buck Dr
Pine Haven WY 82721

Call Sign: KF6ADZ
Robert W Angell
28 Lake Cort Dr
Pine Haven WY
827219796

Call Sign: KF6LWE
George E Cox
32 Lake Court Dr
Pine Haven WY 82721

Call Sign: WO7L
James D Noecker
17 Vista Grande Dr
Pine Haven WY 82721

Call Sign: WB0YEX
Lynn E Holden
Box 687
Pinedale WY 82941

Call Sign: WS7X
Loren H Denney
1122 N Crear Ln
Pinedale WY 829410723

Call Sign: N7TBV
Samuel B Martin
115 Redstone New Fork
River Rd
Pinedale WY 829413020

Call Sign: W7VHS
Ralph V Cole
221 S Maybelle Ave
Pinedale WY 82941

Call Sign: KE7NPJ
Alexander M Mak
11 W Buffalo
Pinedale WY 829412163

Call Sign: KE7OOY
Jeffrey M Mak
11 W Buffalo St
Pinedale WY 829412163

Call Sign: KD7PNH
Spencer M Hartman
Pinedale WY 82941

Call Sign: KD7CGY
Ernest W Kawa
Pinedale WY 82941

Call Sign: KD7OLI
Robert J Laing
Pinedale WY 82941

Call Sign: KD7CXC
Eileen A Manzanedo
Pinedale WY 82941

Call Sign: KE6JIN
Randall Peterson
Pinedale WY 82941

Call Sign: WB5CNM
Randall M Williams
Pinedale WY 82941

Call Sign: KE7RWV
David M Smith
Pinedale WY 82941

Call Sign: KF7GPG
Jon D Gibson
Pinedale WY 829412377

Call Sign: KF7QND
Joshua D Anderson
Pinedale WY 82941

Call Sign: KB7EMS
Larry D Yack
Pinedale WY 82941

Call Sign: KC7UBZ
Roy Bryan
429 12 Sunlight Dr
Powell WY 82435

Call Sign: KC7UCA
Sonja F Bryan
429 12 Sunlight Dr
Powell WY 82435

Call Sign: KC7UAM
Tyler T Foster
5th St Apt D

Powell WY 82435

Call Sign: KB7JUU
Marlitt H Halstead
561 Ave C
Powell WY 82435

Call Sign: KB0SCI
Adam C Allen
519 Ave E
Powell WY 82435

Call Sign: KF7BXS
Thomas H Hooper
506 Avenue B
Powell WY 82435

Call Sign: K7EMS
Robert H Elder
565 Avenue B
Powell WY 824350053

Call Sign: K7KD
Carol J Jaussaud
134 Clover Dr
Powell WY 82435

Call Sign: KA7TSQ
Patrick H Brennan
885 Davis Rd
Powell WY 82435

Call Sign: N7YGS
Carrol A Johnson
885 Davis Rd
Powell WY 82435

Call Sign: W7QNS
Dave L Johnson
885 Davis Rd
Powell WY 82435

Call Sign: WA7QNS
Dave L Johnson
885 Davis Rd

Powell WY 82435

Call Sign: KF7EB
Harold W Wolfe
473 E 8th St
Powell WY 82435

Call Sign: KD7BXA
Jim D Johnson
411 E Jefferson
Powell WY 82435

Call Sign: WA2IZL
Calvin A Jeanroy
511 Hwy 114
Powell WY 82435

Call Sign: AA7YH
Dale C Oursler
861 Lanc 11
Powell WY 82435

Call Sign: KE7CCR
Harley W Wassink
1057 Lane 11 1/2 Box 308
Powell WY 824350308

Call Sign: WD8ASA
Gary E Szatkowski
1735 Lane 14
Powell WY 82435

Call Sign: WB0BQI
Edward E Miller
760 Lane 9H
Powell WY 82435

Call Sign: K2JN
John D Carlini
17 Little Rock Rd
Powell WY 824358143

Call Sign: KC7ZRQ
Carl L Glass
1272 Ln 10

Powell WY 82435

Call Sign: WB3EJQ
William J Ruth Jr
1 Louis Lamour Ln
Powell WY 82435

Call Sign: KF7ITY
Richard W Lyke Jr
49 Montar Rd
Powell WY 82435

Call Sign: KC7UUP
Keith L Wells
355 N Absaroka
Powell WY 82435

Call Sign: KD7HPJ
Bryan Kieft
215 N Ferris St
Powell WY 82435

Call Sign: KI6NTI
Dan Liggett
PO Box 1257
Powell WY 82435

Call Sign: K5PAA
Edward E Mitchell
17 Rd 1 Ab
Powell WY 82435

Call Sign: KB7GPH
Linda N Mitchell
17 Rd 1 Ab
Powell WY 82435

Call Sign: KB7FER
Cody J Vincent
855 Rd 10
Powell WY 82435

Call Sign: KJ6OEQ
Timothy S Delinger
769 Rd 11

Powell WY 82435

Call Sign: KD6AKD
Janet L Parker
1347 Rd 20
Powell WY 82435

Call Sign: AC6CV
Melvin C Parker
1347 Rd 20
Powell WY 82435

Call Sign: W5RCW
Alvin E Robinson
725 Rd 5
Powell WY 82435

Call Sign: K7ALR
C David Miller
465 Rd 8
Powell WY 82435

Call Sign: KD7ROP
C David Miller
465 Rd 8
Powell WY 82435

Call Sign: KF7DPO
Elisabeth R Liggett
1060 Rd 8
Powell WY 82435

Call Sign: KF7DPP
Stephanie G Liggett
1060 Rd 8
Powell WY 82435

Call Sign: W7CQN
Manuel E Olveda
813 Rd 8 1/2 Rt 3
Powell WY 82435

Call Sign: W7EM
Everett H Marine
836 Riverside Dr

Powell WY 82435

Call Sign: W7SDA
Chester C Stanwaity
353 S Ferris St
Powell WY 82435

Call Sign: KB7JUT
Kenneth M Koski
437 S Hamilton
Powell WY 82435

Call Sign: WA7IXH
Dean R Baker Sr
442 Sunlight Dr
Powell WY 82435

Call Sign: KD7KYI
David H Blevins
425 Sunlight Dr
Powell WY 82435

Call Sign: KC7ISR
Alfred L Clark
Powell WY 82435

Call Sign: K7SUB
Robert V Grater
Powell WY 824350822

Call Sign: KB0YKM
Mark Liggett
Powell WY 82435

Call Sign: W7WIR
Brian J Thompson
Powell WY 82435

Call Sign: KE7ZEZ
Dan Liggett
Powell WY 82435

Call Sign: W7EMI
Dan Liggett
Powell WY 82435

Call Sign: W5EMF
Mark Liggett
Powell WY 82435

Call Sign: KD7VLI
Roy O Gregory
Powell WY 82435

FCC Amateur Radio Licenses in Ralston

Call Sign: KC7FLY
Kelly J Burgener
Box 691
Ralston WY 82440

FCC Amateur Radio Licenses in Ranchester

Call Sign: K7BA
William C Robinson
Box 378
Ranchester WY 82839

Call Sign: KA0OCJ
Larry J Swartzendruber
135 Wolf Creek Rd
Ranchester WY 82839

Call Sign: KA7CPT
Robert B Dalton
Ranchester WY 82839

Call Sign: W7IEG
Robert N Jacobson
Ranchester WY 82839

Call Sign: WB7TBH
Robert J Spicer
Ranchester WY 82839

Call Sign: KF7QQQ
Jesse D Maslowski
Ranchester WY 82839

FCC Amateur Radio Licenses in Rawlins

Call Sign: KC7DDQ
Tommy J Karnes
918 14th St
Rawlins WY 82301

Call Sign: KB7RDB
David W Huddleston
548 15th St Apt 105
Rawlins WY 823015256

Call Sign: KA7SGN
Ray L Todd
617 5th
Rawlins WY 82301

Call Sign: KA7SGP
Vani Bjork
620 5th St
Rawlins WY 82301

Call Sign: KJ7AZ
Timothy G Taylor
213 7th
Rawlins WY 82301

Call Sign: W7KF
William M Kangas
Box 1122
Rawlins WY 82301

Call Sign: WA7LFT
Robert T Patterson
Box 1444
Rawlins WY 82301

Call Sign: W7GBG
Gerald M Smith
2427 Dunblane Dr
Rawlins WY 82301

Call Sign: N7ZED

Ted J Garcia Sr
501 E Davis
Rawlins WY 82301

Call Sign: N7ZEE
George A Jordan Jr
217 E Jeffers Dr
Rawlins WY 82301

Call Sign: KD7HAT
Tori Adams
714 E Murray St
Rawlins WY 82301

Call Sign: KE0NP
Robert E Flanagan
1411 Edinburgh St Apt
313
Rawlins WY 82301

Call Sign: KC7IMC
Timothy S Bjork
224 El Rancho Dr
Rawlins WY 82301

Call Sign: KC7RZI
Myron K Fults
1916 Elm
Rawlins WY 82301

Call Sign: KC7RZJ
Rita M Fults
1916 Elm
Rawlins WY 82301

Call Sign: KD7HAS
Robert L Smith
2410 Inverness
Rawlins WY 82301

Call Sign: N7ZEG
Douglas L Smith
2423 Kilmary
Rawlins WY 82301

Call Sign: KF7CXK
Kirk D Sherman
2520 Kilmary Dr
Rawlins WY 82301

Call Sign: W7REV
Kirk D Sherman
2520 Kilmary Dr
Rawlins WY 82301

Call Sign: WB7TMT
William I Shaffer
301 La Paloma Dr
Rawlins WY 82301

Call Sign: KD7LTK
Thomas K Cook
199 Los Altos Dr
Rawlins WY 82301

Call Sign: KC7PFQ
Kenneth J Klapatch
1820 Mactavish Ct Apt
115
Rawlins WY 82301

Call Sign: KC7OZU
Carbon County Amateur
Radio Club
305 Mc Micken
Rawlins WY 82301

Call Sign: NN7H
Duane V Shillinger
305 Mc Micken St
Rawlins WY 82301

Call Sign: K7YCQ
Richard J Fassett
1310 Mountain View Blvd
Rawlins WY 83201

Call Sign: N7ODI
Rosalie M Fassett
1310 Mountain View Blvd

Rawlins WY 82301

Call Sign: N7WTW
Kelly K Hunt
1333 Mt View
Rawlins WY 82301

Call Sign: KF6VQO
Michael Brucato Jr
1017 N Jeffers Dr
Rawlins WY 82301

Call Sign: WB7NIJ
David W Morris
624 Ryan St
Rawlins WY 82301

Call Sign: WB7SYJ
Patricia A Morris
624 Ryan St
Rawlins WY 82301

Call Sign: KD7JJA
Edwin R Henderson
610 Third St
Rawlins WY 82301

Call Sign: KC7AAI
Jeffery D Campbell
1212 Veterans Ave
Rawlins WY 82301

Call Sign: KA7ZKI
Kevin P Reeves
608 W State
Rawlins WY 82301

Call Sign: KB7MPF
Eileen Miller
1205 W Walnut
Rawlins WY 82301

Call Sign: KB1BWZ
David M Noll
Rawlins WY 82301

| FCC Amateur Radio |
| Licenses in Riverton |

Call Sign: KC7RGZ
Matthew E King Sr
119 Apache Ave
Riverton WY 82501

Call Sign: KD7WUS
Amanda P Stanl
2 Big Bear
Riverton WY 82501

Call Sign: KA7PHM
Richard P Winslow
Box 2482
Riverton WY 82501

Call Sign: WB7FFK
Frank J Moore
26 Burma Rd
Riverton WY 82501

Call Sign: KB7JHN
Gerald W Flamang
240 Burma Rd
Riverton WY 82501

Call Sign: KD7BN
Lawrence P Hudson
250 Burma Rd
Riverton WY 82501

Call Sign: N7EMI
Merlene R Hudson
250 Burma Rd
Riverton WY 82501

Call Sign: KB7HLI
John C Dunlap
35 Creek Dr
Riverton WY 82501

Call Sign: KF7BZZ

John W Mercer Jr
63 Dodrill Rd
Riverton WY 82501

Call Sign: W7XK
John W Mercer Jr
63 Dodrill Rd
Riverton WY 82501

Call Sign: WF7LSU
John W Mercer Jr
63 Dodrill Rd
Riverton WY 82501

Call Sign: KC7UUN
Charles L Cliame
1324 E Adams
Riverton WY 82501

Call Sign: KC7QWY
Mike L Kappus
909 E Jackson
Riverton WY 82501

Call Sign: KD7MTF
Michael D Warren
915 E Lincoln
Riverton WY 82501

Call Sign: KE7XC
Donald L Rood Sr
210 E Lincoln Ave
Riverton WY 82501

Call Sign: KD7MTE
Paul E Eells
521 E Lincoln Ave
Riverton WY 82501

Call Sign: KC0MVD
Edward J Gross III
1213 E Main St Apt 1
Riverton WY 82501

Call Sign: N7PPG

Leo J Beck Jr
121 E Park
Riverton WY 82501

Steven A Carpenter
71 Lost Wells Cir
Riverton WY 82501

Robert M Sackett
318 N 5th W
Riverton WY 82501

Call Sign: W7NKR
Ralph G Schaefer Jr
505 E Park
Riverton WY 82501

Call Sign: KA7GPN
Mark O Harris
49 Miller Ln
Riverton WY 82501

Call Sign: KC7ITG
Joseph B Sullivan
1629 N 8th St W
Riverton WY 82501

Call Sign: KC7YWY
Richard A Strous
1618 E Park
Riverton WY 82501

Call Sign: W7MOH
Mark O Harris
49 Miller Ln
Riverton WY 82501

Call Sign: KB7JHP
Josh R Beckman
839 Northpoint Circle
Riverton WY 82501

Call Sign: KA0NDS
Paul A Wardner
103 E Park Avenue
Riverton WY 82501

Call Sign: KB7BIM
Robert J Stange
59 Minter Ln
Riverton WY 82501

Call Sign: N7DMO
James F Kelliher
440 Nth 4th W Apt C
Riverton WY 82501

Call Sign: KB7EGZ
Neal W Kramer
927 Eastview
Riverton WY 82501

Call Sign: AD9V
Richard W Hardt
62 Minter Ln
Riverton WY 82501

Call Sign: KB7WOL
Scott E Luers
324 Oak Ln
Riverton WY 82501

Call Sign: KB7WXO
Joyce A Keldsen
900 Forest Dr Apt A2
Riverton WY 82501

Call Sign: N7HYE
Robert P Connelly
75 Minter Ln
Riverton WY 82501

Call Sign: N7TSP
Lonny A Fairfield
74 Peterson Rd
Riverton WY 82501

Call Sign: KC7BNC
Chuck W Hoelzen
1 Grandview Ct
Riverton WY 82501

Call Sign: KC7WZZ
Steven A Hixson
306 N 16th St E
Riverton WY 82501

Call Sign: N7PGR
Darren W Kreklow
1106 Pinecrest St
Riverton WY 82501

Call Sign: KB7EUN
David G Hambrick
374 Granite Circle
Riverton WY 82501

Call Sign: K0FOP
Jon W Springer
340 N 5th St E
Riverton WY 82501

Call Sign: KD7DLZ
Loral D Verhoeven
261 Raintree Dr
Riverton WY 825019330

Call Sign: W7NFL
David G Hambrick
216 Heather Dr
Riverton WY 82501

Call Sign: KF7GHY
Jon W Springer
340 N 5th St E
Riverton WY 82501

Call Sign: KD7GQN
Ralph A Estell Jr
320 Ramshorn Dr
Riverton WY 82501

Call Sign: KC7ZVV

Call Sign: KB7EEQ

Call Sign: KD7OGO

William K Spillman
259 Rendezvous Rd
Riverton WY 82501

Call Sign: N7UOG
Elaine J Patterson
3555 Riverside Dr
Riverton WY 82501

Call Sign: N7TZF
Willis R Patterson
3555 Riverside Dr
Riverton WY 82501

Call Sign: KD7UZI
Christopher N Jones
1336 Robin Ln
Riverton WY 82501

Call Sign: KD7WKI
James C Dalley
3 Roundup Rd
Riverton WY 82501

Call Sign: KB5JR
Boyd L Potts
1315 S Federal Blvd 55
Riverton WY 82501

Call Sign: W7BKH
Jay R Hunter
209 Shamrock
Riverton WY 82501

Call Sign: KA7WNO
Bill E Carpenter
224 Shamrock
Riverton WY 82501

Call Sign: KD7JXC
Jim P Anderson
510 Spire Dr
Riverton WY 82501

Call Sign: KA7IAJ

Thomas L Stocks
418 Summit Dr
Riverton WY 825014017

Call Sign: KD7IL
Roger A Hicks
1155 W Mountain View
Dr
Riverton WY 82501

Call Sign: KB7KXN
William D Snapp
617 W Park Ave
Riverton WY 82501

Call Sign: KE5KTX
Andrew P Mcneel
1625 W Park Ave 1
Riverton WY 82501

Call Sign: KB7GOZ
Harold A Macon
225 W Sunset
Riverton WY 82501

Call Sign: KD7UJL
Harold A Macon
225 W Sunset
Riverton WY 82501

Call Sign: N7DAH
Gary L Carlson
923 Westview Dr
Riverton WY 82501

Call Sign: KE7JZS
James L Masters
42 Whitetail Dr
Riverton WY 82501

Call Sign: N7WSD
Franklin G Asmundson
Riverton WY 82501

Call Sign: KB7SPV

Joseph A Pedersen
Riverton WY 82501

Call Sign: W7VFV
Floyd C Anderson
Riverton WY 82501

Call Sign: K7YJX
Sam M Iiams
Riverton WY 82501

Call Sign: KB7YWJ
James F Sandt Sr
Riverton WY 82501

Call Sign: WW4MM
David J Warrington
Riverton WY 825011929

FCC Amateur Radio Licenses in Robertson

Call Sign: W7DMD
Don L Griffin
Robertson WY 82944

Call Sign: N7TFT
Marilyn K Griffin
Robertson WY 82944

Call Sign: KF7OOC
Carol A Kennedy
Robertson WY 82944

FCC Amateur Radio Licenses in Rock River

Call Sign: WY0MN
Lex A Heath
Rock River WY 82083

FCC Amateur Radio Licenses in Rock Springs

Call Sign: N7VSC

Robert B Wilcock
636 4th Ave W
Rock Springs WY 82901

Call Sign: KE7UUJ
Steven I Rizzi
1032 7th St
Rock Springs WY 82901

Call Sign: AC7AF
Brian L Roberts
1234 9th Apt 1
Rock Springs WY 82901

Call Sign: N7ABC
Johnny R Ramirez
1349 Alpine St
Rock Springs WY 82901

Call Sign: AC7HW
Alan R Kirsch
1660 Blair Ave 61
Rock Springs WY 82901

Call Sign: KA7NKQ
Alan R Kirsch
1660 Blair Ave 61
Rock Springs WY 82901

Call Sign: NO7J
Robert L Anderson
Box 1288
Rock Springs WY 82901

Call Sign: KE7IGK
Nathan T Martin
800 Burr Dr
Rock Springs WY 82901

Call Sign: N7OQP
Gary D Valentine
818 Bushnell Ave
Rock Springs WY 82901

Call Sign: N7RUG

Judy A Valentine
818 Bushnell Avenue
Rock Springs WY
829017204

Call Sign: KB7WXV
George R Hanrahan Jr
1514 Carbon Cir
Rock Springs WY
829017307

Call Sign: KD7CJO
Robert J Spain
2475 Cascade Dr 201
Rock Springs WY 82901

Call Sign: KA7RMS
Albert C Emden
240 Cherokee Dr
Rock Springs WY 82901

Call Sign: K7KX
Bryan D Whitcomb
501 Coldwater Creek Dr
Rock Springs WY 82901

Call Sign: N1SJT
Jane E Fillmore
1512 Collins St
Rock Springs WY 82901

Call Sign: KB7HEP
Allen P Hafner
106 Community Park Dr
Rock Springs WY 82901

Call Sign: N7IUQ
Andrew C Conde
706.5 Dewar Dr
Rock Springs WY 82901

Call Sign: KB7ZEH
Jason M Shakle
1650 Dewar Dr 148
Rock Springs WY 82901

Call Sign: KB7LUT
Jeremy M Weber
1117 Divide St
Rock Springs WY 82901

Call Sign: KB7BEN
Richard B Weber
1117 Divide St
Rock Springs WY 82901

Call Sign: KF7URS
Patrick J Lacey
1700 Donalynn Dr Lot 28
Rock Springs WY 82901

Call Sign: K7DRA
David R Allman Sr
1300 Eagle Way
Rock Springs WY 82901

Call Sign: ND5B
David R Allman Sr
1300 Eaglc Way
Rock Springs WY 82901

Call Sign: KC7OTB
Jamie Call
812 Eisenhower Dr
Rock Springs WY 82901

Call Sign: N7PHN
Kristy Call
812 Eisenhower Dr
Rock Springs WY 82901

Call Sign: KE7FGA
Joann L Gustke
627 Euclid
Rock Springs WY 82901

Call Sign: KD7GVV
Grant W Bawden
525 Evelyn Rd
Rock Springs WY 82901

Rock Springs WY 82901

Call Sign: KB7PJW
Talia F Deccio
2024 Fir Dr
Rock Springs WY 82901

Call Sign: N7NGT
Shauna A Peters Richards
2024 Fir Dr
Rock Springs WY 82901

Call Sign: KB7NYQ
Crystal A Richards
2024 Fir Dr
Rock Springs WY 82901

Call Sign: N7NGS
Johanna Richards
2024 Fir Dr
Rock Springs WY 82901

Call Sign: KR7J
Kerry W Richards
2024 Fir Dr
Rock Springs WY 82901

Call Sign: KC7MVC
Shara K Richards
2024 Fir Dr
Rock Springs WY 82901

Call Sign: KC7MVB
Zach S Richards
2024 Fir Dr
Rock Springs WY 82901

Call Sign: KD7GQM
Donald L Nuzum Jr
222 Gateway Blvd 49
Rock Springs WY 82901

Call Sign: KC7MKY
Harriet A Muir
40 Hillcrest Ln
Rock Springs WY 82901

Call Sign: KB7PND
Kennith A Muir
40 Hillcrest Ln
Rock Springs WY 82901

Call Sign: N0CY
Cecil D Mc Coy
340 Hillcrest Ln
Rock Springs WY 82901

Call Sign: KA7FIT
Phyllis I Mc Coy
340 Hillcrest Ln
Rock Springs WY
829012906

Call Sign: KF7SMA
Steven S Powell
521 I St
Rock Springs WY 82901

Call Sign: KE5WI
Charles D Crawford
241 Jade St
Rock Springs WY 82901

Call Sign: KA7KKG
Douglas A Telck
1501 James Dr
Rock Springs WY 82901

Call Sign: KF7HIL
Billy Lew
1326 Juniper Dr
Rock Springs WY 82901

Call Sign: KF7ILS
Anthony R Lew
1326 Juniper Dr
Rock Springs WY 82901

Call Sign: KF7ILR
Timothy M Lew
1326 Juniper Dr

Call Sign: KF7OBL
Patricia J Kappes
285 Kappes Rd
Rock Springs WY 82901

Call Sign: KE7FPK
Sienna D Merchant
117 L Apt 4
Rock Springs WY 82901

Call Sign: K7EEP
Edward E Patterson
22 Lakota Dr
Rock Springs WY 82902

Call Sign: KF7URU
Peter J Foran
515 Ludvig St
Rock Springs WY 82901

Call Sign: N7NLZ
John D Jacovitch
725 Massachusetts Ave
Rock Springs WY 82901

Call Sign: KC7SDM
Michael J Lehman
402 Monarch Ct
Rock Springs WY 82901

Call Sign: KF7CJE
Hubert H Hazelett
226 Mountain Rd
Rock Springs WY 82901

Call Sign: KD7CIH
Iker Torrontegui
820 Muir Ave
Rock Springs WY 82901

Call Sign: N7UIA
Douglas K Barker
1230 Palisades Way

Rock Springs WY 82901

Call Sign: KB7HEQ
Doris I Haskell
1403 Palisades Way
Rock Springs WY 82901

Call Sign: KF7SLY
Gary R Bourrette
255 Polk St
Rock Springs WY 82901

Call Sign: K7TSS
John P Montz Sr
211 R St
Rock Springs WY 82901

Call Sign: N7WIN
Todd W Steffensmeier
510 S Main
Rock Springs WY 82901

Call Sign: KE7GPK
John W Aaron III
3143 Scott Dr
Rock Springs WY 82901

Call Sign: KD7IJT
Roger Tyler
398 Turret Dr
Rock Springs WY 82901

Call Sign: KB7LGV
Angela D White
1101 View St
Rock Springs WY 82901

Call Sign: W7LSM
Leo S Miloff
1620 W 2nd St 24
Rock Springs WY
829017659

Call Sign: WB7ENZ
Leo S Miloff

1620 W 2nd St 24
Rock Springs WY
829017659

Call Sign: AA0FI
David E Rose
1620 W 2nd St Lot 2
Rock Springs WY 82901

Call Sign: KB5MKS
Edward E Patterson
935 Walnut
Rock Springs WY 82902

Call Sign: KD7DUC
Michael H Miller
478 Washakie Dr
Rock Springs WY 82901

Call Sign: KD7NWN
Kent C Mccort
2625 Westridge Dr
Rock Springs WY 82901

Call Sign: N7MGI
Linda J Call
2324 Westviev Ave
Rock Springs WY 82901

Call Sign: N7MGG
Howard S Call
2324 Westview Ave
Rock Springs WY 82901

Call Sign: KF7PDQ
Charles E Pridmore
224 Wild Rose Ln
Rock Springs WY 82901

Call Sign: KB7MXG
Jennifer Eyring
Rock Springs WY 82902

Call Sign: W7JH
John M Henderson

Rock Springs WY 82902

Call Sign: KB7WWN
Kenneth E Howard Sr
Rock Springs WY 82902

Call Sign: WY7U
Sweetwater Amateur
Radio Club
Rock Springs WY 82902

Call Sign: WB9HZQ
Mark O Thompson
Rock Springs WY 82902

Call Sign: AA7EM
Gerald J Bracken
Rock Springs WY
829020573

Call Sign: KB7WWL
Charles M Clausen
Rock Springs WY 82902

Call Sign: AA7SZ
Donald E Wolfe
Rock Springs WY
829021054

Call Sign: N8SZ
Donald E Wolfe
Rock Springs WY
829021054

Call Sign: KE7OVK
James M Glennon
Rock Springs WY
829020584

**FCC Amateur Radio
Licenses in Rolling Hills**

Call Sign: NB7I
Kenneth J Link
66 S Coyote Rd

Rolling Hills WY 82637

FCC Amateur Radio Licenses in Rozet

Call Sign: WB6IAJ
Karolyn S Jones
13358 Hwy 51
Rozet WY 82727

Call Sign: KD7YLV
Timothy L Hughes
28 Irene St Adon Rt
Rozet WY 82727

Call Sign: K7CWM
Charles W Messenheimer
186 N Heptner Rd
Rozet WY 82727

Call Sign: KF7CBG
Walter S Campbell
40 Oneal Circle
Rozet WY 82727

Call Sign: WY7WSC
Walter S Campbell
40 Oneal Circle
Rozet WY 82727

Call Sign: KE7NBE
Charles W Messenheimer
Timber Creek Rd
Rozet WY 82727

FCC Amateur Radio Licenses in Saratoga

Call Sign: WB7TJP
Greg C Ryan
Box 189
Saratoga WY 82331

Call Sign: N7GCR
Greg C Ryan

Box 189
Saratoga WY 82331

Call Sign: KD7UFR
Arthur W Dahlke
CR 550
Saratoga WY 82331

Call Sign: KK7HP
Robert Q Hewitt
112 Pickpike Rd
Saratoga WY 823310704

Call Sign: KA7SGS
Ellen M Burgess
St Rt Box 9N Ryan Park
Saratoga WY 82331

Call Sign: N5LDP
D Ron Campbell
Saratoga WY 82331

Call Sign: KC7NFP
David P Holt
Saratoga WY 82331

Call Sign: KA7SGR
Ella V Young
Saratoga WY 82331

Call Sign: KF7JPX
Joseph B Gaudesi
Saratoga WY 82331

FCC Amateur Radio Licenses in Shell

Call Sign: AC7MI
David A Cook
3120 Highline Dr
Shell WY 824410123

Call Sign: N6EHM
David A Cook
3120 Highline Dr

Shell WY 824410123

Call Sign: AK7MD
David A Cook
3210 Highline Dr
Shell WY 824410123

FCC Amateur Radio Licenses in Sheridan

Call Sign: KB7DGW
Dan F Sherman
1122 5th Ave E
Sheridan WY 82801

Call Sign: WB7N
Dan F Sherman
1122 5th Ave E
Sheridan WY 82801

Call Sign: KB7NDV
Brian K Musgrave
930 5th St
Sheridan WY 82801

Call Sign: N7GYA
Raymond L Kent
1032 6th Ave E
Sheridan WY 82801

Call Sign: KA6ALK
Mark D Elledge
1226 6th Ave E
Sheridan WY 82801

Call Sign: K7KPH
Mark D Elledge
1226 6th Ave E
Sheridan WY 82801

Call Sign: KF7FVQ
Mark D Elledge
1226 6th Ave E
Sheridan WY 82801

Call Sign: WB7AHJ
James E Coombs
410 Adkin St
Sheridan WY 82801

Call Sign: WA1VLF
Marjorie L Carter
503 Canby
Sheridan WY 82801

Call Sign: KE7AYV
John B Todd
5901 Coffeen Ave 7
Sheridan WY 82801

Call Sign: N7WYN
Eric A Peterson
418 Adkins Pl
Sheridan WY 82801

Call Sign: KF7LFR
Steven B Waddell
753 Carrington St
Sheridan WY 82801

Call Sign: N7KEO
Henry E Sickler Jr
44 Cox Valley Rd
Sheridan WY 82801

Call Sign: N7XPM
Sandra J Peterson
418 Adkins Pl
Sheridan WY 82801

Call Sign: WA9HQV
Craig G Vogt
27 Cato Dr
Sheridan WY 82801

Call Sign: KA7WTT
Mary F Sickler
44 Cox Valley Rd
Sheridan WY 82801

Call Sign: W7QPP
Robert B Miller
129 Bellevue
Sheridan WY 82801

Call Sign: W7JID
Theodore P Strahan
1563 Cedar
Sheridan WY 82801

Call Sign: KE7FPN
Josiah G Miller
1341 Dana
Sheridan WY 82801

Call Sign: W7LRU
Clair L Mc Holland
1432 Big Horn Ave
Sheridan WY 828015508

Call Sign: WA7D
Murry F Clark
1436 Cedar Ave
Sheridan WY 828013422

Call Sign: KD7NLX
Lark A Baker
1615 De Smet
Sheridan WY 82801

Call Sign: KC7DKO
Ronald C Hudson
1704 Big Horn Ave
Sheridan WY 82801

Call Sign: KC7LP
Larry J Tannehill
1436 Cedar Ave
Sheridan WY 82801

Call Sign: N7BMR
Ronald L Martini
1723 Desmet
Sheridan WY 82801

Call Sign: KE7PLK
Marc T Marlowe
1623 Bowman Ave
Sheridan WY 82801

Call Sign: W0GIL
Lindell E Gillam
51 Coffeen Ave
Sheridan WY 82801

Call Sign: W7RSJ
David E Bell
1771 Desmet
Sheridan WY 82801

Call Sign: KA7MSV
Donald T Dellit
Box 3013
Sheridan WY 82801

Call Sign: KJ7VY
David Stine
51 Coffeen Ave
Sheridan WY 82801

Call Sign: KD7QOO
Justin Q Carlson
2519 Dry Ranch Rd
Sheridan WY 82801

Call Sign: NY7A
Timothy C Lanham
616 Broadway
Sheridan WY 82801

Call Sign: N7HRI
Jonathan D Hansen
5901 Coffeen Ave 28
Sheridan WY 82801

Call Sign: N6PQO
Walker K Burton
532 E Brundage St
Sheridan WY 82801

Call Sign: KE7MK
Ric A Epperle
730 E Heald
Sheridan WY 82801

Call Sign: KC0UWI
Tony J Diaz
315 E Loucks St
Sheridan WY 82801

Call Sign: KE7HUY
Tony J Diaz
315 E Loucks St
Sheridan WY 82801

Call Sign: KE7MDC
Tony J Diaz
315 E Loucks St
Sheridan WY 82801

Call Sign: KD8CSA
Todd M Prout
2057 Frackelton St
Sheridan WY 82801

Call Sign: KF7CAC
Todd M Prout
2057 Frackelton St
Sheridan WY 82801

Call Sign: K7GR
Gene G Roelfsema
1477 Hillpond Dr
Sheridan WY 828012166

Call Sign: KE7UJD
William M Campbell
1 Home Ranch Circle
Sheridan WY 82801

Call Sign: KB0SUM
Jeff A Grimes
30 Home Ranch Circle
Sheridan WY 82801

Call Sign: WB7VEL
James M Livingston
603 Huntington St
Sheridan WY 82801

Call Sign: W7TZK
Timothy R Koenig
53 Hwy 335
Sheridan WY 82801

Call Sign: W7BDN
Bruce D Nolting
207 Idaho Ave
Sheridan WY 82801

Call Sign: KF7KNK
Linda M Nolting
207 Idaho Ave
Sheridan WY 82801

Call Sign: KE7NPE
Bruce D Nolting
207 Idaho Ave
Sheridan WY 82801

Call Sign: K7RFL
George Cherni
955 Illinois
Sheridan WY 82801

Call Sign: KF7SQO
Dennis A Ross
1254 Illinois Ave
Sheridan WY 82801

Call Sign: W7ABO
Victor R Hewett
552 Kallua
Sheridan WY 82801

Call Sign: N7OCH
Danial W Bousa
958 Kentucky Ave 7
Sheridan WY 82801

Call Sign: WJ7K
Linda S Spear
926 La Clede
Sheridan WY 82801

Call Sign: W7GUX
Sheridan Radio Amateur
League Inc
926 La Clede St
Sheridan WY 82801

Call Sign: WB7NVR
Larry A Andre
854 Leopard St
Sheridan WY 82801

Call Sign: WA7YZO
David J Dolecheck
582 Long Dr
Sheridan WY 82801

Call Sign: K7TOT
Ross K Peterson
446 Lower Prairie Dog
Sheridan WY 82801

Call Sign: KE7UDK
Ross K Peterson
446 Lower Prairie Dog
Sheridan WY 82801

Call Sign: N7BXY
William P Gleason
1271 Marion
Sheridan WY 82801

Call Sign: KB7IWZ
Ronald D Weaver
659 Marion St
Sheridan WY 82801

Call Sign: WA7SGG
Charles L Fike
7 Maxine Pl
Sheridan WY 82801

Call Sign: KN2QWO
Robert E Grimmer Sr
379 Meade Creek Rd
Sheridan WY 82801

Call Sign: N7WQQ
Dorothy E Chapman
17 N Badger
Sheridan WY 82801

Call Sign: KF7DRH
Cloud Peak Radio &
Electronics Group
1726 N Main St
Sheridan WY 82801

Call Sign: WY7SHR
Cloud Peak Radio &
Electronics Group
1726 N Main St
Sheridan WY 82801

Call Sign: KD7TKL
Joseph A Romlein
1909 N Main St Apt 9
Sheridan WY 82801

Call Sign: KB7AAY
Duane C Buchholz
1567 N Mountain View Dr
Sheridan WY 82801

Call Sign: KD8NBN
James M Terwilliger
601 N Sheridan Ave
Sheridan WY 82801

Call Sign: W7LLP
Walter A Crook
867 Olympus Dr
Sheridan WY 82801

Call Sign: N7WYR
Judith M Faurot

18 Paradise Dr
Sheridan WY 82801

Call Sign: N7WYO
Robert L Faurot
18 Paradise Dr
Sheridan WY 82801

Call Sign: WA0UQE
Carl D Cordell
47 Red Fox Dr
Sheridan WY 82801

Call Sign: N7WYP
Ann B Van Trump
101 Red Fox Dr
Sheridan WY 82801

Call Sign: N7YRJ
Lonnie L Van Trump
101 Red Fox Dr
Sheridan WY 82801

Call Sign: KB7DGX
Braddon M Van Slyke
273 S Badger
Sheridan WY 82801

Call Sign: WR7S
Kenneth R Humphrey
232 S Jeferson St
Sheridan WY 82801

Call Sign: KD7SIW
Jane E Wohl
631 S Jefferson
Sheridan WY 82801

Call Sign: WT7T
Barry M Wohl
631 S Jefferson St
Sheridan WY 82801

Call Sign: KB7TVU
Susan E Berberick

433 S Main 5
Sheridan WY 82801

Call Sign: KA7ACM
John F Berberick
433 S Main St Apt 5
Sheridan WY 82801

Call Sign: KA7EHG
Henry E Sickler Sr
2076 S Sheridan Ave Apt
208
Sheridan WY 82801

Call Sign: K7CQO
Nels A Nelson III
606 S Thurmond
Sheridan WY 82801

Call Sign: N7XPK
Milton L Liming
1170 S Thurmond
Sheridan WY 82801

Call Sign: WB7THJ
Roland E Schoenborn
108 S Thurmond St
Sheridan WY 82801

Call Sign: W7PMA
Bradford J Spear
104 Scott Dr
Sheridan WY 828013249

Call Sign: KC7CHD
Catherine J Kusel
532 Soldier Creek Rd
Sheridan WY 82801

Call Sign: KF7PHQ
Patrick W Lawson
99 State Hwy 335
Sheridan WY 82801

Call Sign: N4CHW

Gale W Cleven
1605 Sugarland Dr
Sheridan WY 82801

Call Sign: AA5XJ
Gary V Morton
2076 Summit Dr
Sheridan WY 82801

Call Sign: KF7UYP
Garet V Morton
2076 Summit Dr
Sheridan WY 82801

Call Sign: WB7DVT
Steven R Schlicting
78 Swaim Rd
Sheridan WY 828018920

Call Sign: WY0PMP
Tony J Diaz
18 Timm Pl
Sheridan WY 82801

Call Sign: KF7DZ
Robert D Elmore
53 Valley View Dr
Sheridan WY 82801

Call Sign: KD7SPD
Patrick Mcdowell
1005 Victoria St
Sheridan WY 82801

Call Sign: N7WYQ
Robert A Waurio
1241 W 11th St
Sheridan WY 82801

Call Sign: WB7EJQ
Brian J Johnson
657 W 13th St 4
Sheridan WY 82801

Call Sign: WA7MGT

Chan J Geer
41 W 7th
Sheridan WY 82801

Call Sign: WA7MGU
Mary A Geer
41 W 7th
Sheridan WY 82801

Call Sign: KF7PHN
Elizabeth A Cherni
377 W Whitney
Sheridan WY 82801

Call Sign: K7CDL
Rondall E Swart
377 W Whitney St
Sheridan WY 82801

Call Sign: KF7CBZ
Rondall E Swart
377 W Whitney St
Sheridan WY 82801

Call Sign: K7LIZ
Elizabeth A Cherni
377 W Whitney St
Sheridan WY 82801

Call Sign: W6RZL
Richard H Hoeck
574 W Works
Sheridan WY 82801

Call Sign: KB7HS
Jack D Maxted
1950 Walnut Ave
Sheridan WY 82801

Call Sign: KB7VCZ
Jeffrey C Baum
15 Whitetail Ln
Sheridan WY 82801

Call Sign: KC7PXA

William W Ohlson
234 Wyoming Ave
Sheridan WY 82801

Call Sign: N7JZE
Andrew E Sickler
1453 Yonkee
Sheridan WY 82801

Call Sign: NX7Z
Quentin D Vinzant
1549 Yonkee
Sheridan WY 82801

Call Sign: KC7CHF
Brian K Swan
1780 Yonkee Ave
Sheridan WY 82801

Call Sign: N7YYQ
John A Calvert
Sheridan WY 82801

Call Sign: WB9OQM
Joshua R Mathison
Sheridan WY 82801

Call Sign: KB7HQZ
James T Palmer
Sheridan WY 82801

Call Sign: KB7CEZ
Herrick J Aldrich
Sheridan WY 828011486

Call Sign: KC7CHE
Lynn Dellitt
Sheridan WY 82801

Call Sign: N9NLP
David D Hamaker
Sheridan WY 82801

Call Sign: WA7RMP
Donald R Kemp

Sheridan WY 82801

Call Sign: KC5ORX
Glenda Mc Grath
Sheridan WY 82801

Call Sign: KC7GDU
Christopher L Thayer
Sheridan WY 82801

Call Sign: K0GVR
John J Mehlhoff
Sheridan WY 82801

Call Sign: KE7HZS
John J Mehlhoff
Sheridan WY 82801

Call Sign: KV5J
Patrick L Starkey
Sheridan WY 82801

Call Sign: KF7CAB
Vicki L Kemp
Sheridan WY 82801

FCC Amateur Radio Licenses in Shoshoni

Call Sign: WA7SRI
Eugene J De Foe
Shoshoni WY 82649

FCC Amateur Radio Licenses in Sinclair

Call Sign: KA7ZKF
Timothy E Mc Cann
Box 313
Sinclair WY 82334

Call Sign: WA7YWA
Donald A Koeneke
401 N 8th
Sinclair WY 82334

Call Sign: KD7HAQ
Jeffrey A Sanders
208 N 8th St
Sinclair WY 82334

Call Sign: KA7NAB
Dennis F Eckes
100 N 9th
Sinclair WY 82334

Call Sign: N7ZEF
Michale J Reed
PO Box 344
Sinclair WY 82334

Call Sign: K0DJ
Robert W Poirier
Sinclair WY 82334

Call Sign: KD7HXD
Kari M Allison
Sinclair WY 82334

Call Sign: N7RON
Kenneth Y Allison
Sinclair WY 82334

Call Sign: KD7SU
Ronald J Bjork
Sinclair WY 82334

Call Sign: N7IJU
Jody A Eckes
Sinclair WY 82334

Call Sign: N7SEI
Laura E Laurentius
Sinclair WY 823340171

Call Sign: KA7ZKE
George W Mc Cann
Sinclair WY 82334

FCC Amateur Radio Licenses in Smoot

Call Sign: KE7QPO
Andrew J Ortenzio
Smoot WY 83126

Call Sign: KE7QPP
Christine A Ortenzio
Smoot WY 83126

FCC Amateur Radio Licenses in Star Valley Ranch

Call Sign: KF7TBG
Christopher D Snow
Box 7362
Star Valley Ranch WY 83127

Call Sign: W7CDS
Christopher D Snow
Box 7362
Star Valley Ranch WY 83127

Call Sign: KC6VUS
Ron M Greer
Box 7398
Star Valley Ranch WY 83127

FCC Amateur Radio Licenses in Story

Call Sign: N7NIL
Heidi J Stainbrook
Box 295
Story WY 82842

Call Sign: W7IOI
Kendall E Cook
Box 63
Story WY 82842

Call Sign: K7KSA
George A Lunbeck
26 Fish Hatchery Rd Box
88
Story WY 82842

Call Sign: WB7SSV
Phyllis J Lunbeck
26 Fish Hatchery Rd Box
88
Story WY 82842

Call Sign: K7MEL
Melvit G Holtz
Story WY 82842

Call Sign: KA0FCR
Catherine A Howell
Story WY 82842

Call Sign: K7VU
Steven D Schilling
Story WY 82842

Call Sign: KD0BSF
David L Mckinney
Story WY 82842

Call Sign: NE7DM
David L Mckinney
Story WY 828420486

Call Sign: AD7ZY
Gerard M Boone
50 Butch Cassidy St
Sundance WY 82729

Call Sign: KD7YYP
Gerard M Boone
50 Butch Cassidy St
Sundance WY 82729

Call Sign: WY7JB
Gerard M Boone
50 Butch Cassidy St
Sundance WY 82729

Call Sign: KC0KAM
Jeff E Mickle
152 Commercial Rd
Sundance WY 82729

Call Sign: N3CMI
Edwin H Hopton Jr
4 Derringer Trl
Sundance WY 827291435

Call Sign: WD9BKQ
Richard Milanowski
659 State Hwy 116
Sundance WY 82729

Call Sign: KA7VBX
Michael J Coy
1011 Warren St
Sundance WY 82729

Call Sign: KA5IDI
John S Mackey
Sundance WY 82729

Call Sign: WY7QP
North East Wy Contest
Association
Sundance WY 827291482

Call Sign: WY7SS
North East Wy Contest
Association
Sundance WY 827291482

Call Sign: KC7DKF
Joann Safford
Sundance WY 82729

Call Sign: KA7VBV

Mary J Wilson
Sundance WY 82729

Call Sign: WY7FD
Dwayne Allen
Sundance WY 827291482

Call Sign: WY7KRA
Katie Allen
Sundance WY 827291482

Call Sign: KF7RJT
Patricia A Boone
Sundance WY 82729

Call Sign: K7VWA
Margaret S Cogdill
Box 103
Ten Sleep WY 82442

Call Sign: W6GJE
Arthur L Smith Jr
Box 184
Ten Sleep WY 82442

Call Sign: KB7WWO
Harvey D Brubaker
3267 E US Hwy 16
Ten Sleep WY 82442

Call Sign: KB7WWM
Virgie Y Brubaker
3267 E US Hwy 16
Ten Sleep WY 82442

Call Sign: N7TMI
Chuck T Irons
Ten Sleep WY 82442

Call Sign: KD7LFI
Curt E Clauson
Box 512
Teton Village WY 83025

Call Sign: W7LMY
Calvin N Mathieu
Teton Village WY 83025

Call Sign: WA3EDQ
Robert S Nuttle
Teton Village WY 83025

Call Sign: KE7GXZ
Michael F Daus
Teton Village WY
830250563

FCC Amateur Radio Licenses in Thayne

Call Sign: WA9YNR
Donald R Cushman
Box 1488
Thayne WY 83127

Call Sign: N7QQL
George A Amussen
88 Brushwood Dr
Thayne WY 83127

Call Sign: KD6DNE
Robert H Smith
161 Country Club Way
Thayne WY 83127

Call Sign: WA7ZIE
Robert K Odle
423 Grizzly Rd
Thayne WY 83127

Call Sign: KE7VNU
Dorothy L Abler
33 Hardman Circle
Thayne WY 83127

Call Sign: KC7VXH
Douglas C Bridenstine
Thayne WY 83127

Call Sign: KC6VSR
Matthew J Clark
Thayne WY 831271156

Call Sign: AH6AJ
Paul G Hanson
Thayne WY 83127

Call Sign: KC7VXG
Orson L Schwab
Thayne WY 83127

Call Sign: KC7DSK
Lonnie A Spencer
Thayne WY 83127

Call Sign: K7DDT
Joel P Abler
Thayne WY 83127

Call Sign: KE7VNT
Joel P Abler
Thayne WY 83127

Call Sign: AD7CG
Matthew J Clark
Thayne WY 831271156

Call Sign: WY7MC
Matthew J Clark
Thayne WY 831271156

FCC Amateur Radio Licenses in Themopolis

Call Sign: AB5JQ
James A Overman
637 Arapahoe
Thermopolis WY 82443

Call Sign: KC5ELJ
Sabrina L Overman
637 Arapahoe St
Thermopolis WY 82443

Call Sign: WZ1D
Paul J Garbin
1310 Arapahoe St
Thermopolis WY 82443

Call Sign: W7VB
Joseph P Ernst
110 Belvedere
Thermopolis WY 82443

Call Sign: AA2GY
Thomas W Farstad
1345 Big Horn St
Thermopolis WY 82443

Call Sign: KC7DLT
Don L Williams
Box 1028
Thermopolis WY
824431028

Call Sign: KJ7AM
Rick L Culp
400 Coyote Run
Thermopolis WY 82443

Call Sign: KD7IDL
Jeremiah W Culp
135 Fremont St
Thermopolis WY 82443

Call Sign: KF7KHL
Maecile Brown
3809 Grass Creek Rd
Thermopolis WY 82443

Call Sign: KD7BAZ
Delbert L Lamoreaux
730 Missouri Flat Rd
Thermopolis WY 82443

Call Sign: KD6EJR
Harvey M Fisher
536 Mondell
Thermopolis WY 82443

Call Sign: KD7RNU
Harvey M Fisher
536 Mondell
Thermopolis WY 82443

Call Sign: KC7KTB
Karlene K King
303 N 7th St
Thermopolis WY 82443

Call Sign: WA7WQC
Edna M Baines
252 N Hwy 20
Thermopolis WY 82443

Call Sign: W7NK
Fred J Baines
252 N Hwy 20
Thermopolis WY
824430008

Call Sign: KB7ZEI
Joseph Nazionale
732 Rd 11
Thermopolis WY 82443

Call Sign: WB2RVE
Robert R Spain
605 S 6th St
Thermopolis WY 82443

Call Sign: N7FJU
Harvey D Seidel
355 S Hwy 20
Thermopolis WY
824430070

Call Sign: KA3ARV
Eugene D Moore

610 Springview
Thermopolis WY 82443

Call Sign: KB7IAH
Carol D Burns
687 Sunny View Dr
Thermopolis WY 82443

Call Sign: N7NCZ
Lee R Burns
687 Sunny View Dr
Thermopolis WY 82443

Call Sign: KB7IAH
Carol D Burns
687 Sunny View Dr
Thermopolis WY 82443

Call Sign: KF7KHM
Carol D Burns
687 Sunny View Dr
Thermopolis WY 82443

Call Sign: WA7JRF
Robert A Overton
682 Sunnyview Dr
Thermopolis WY 82443

Call Sign: N7ZRX
Sherry D Overton
682 Sunnyview Rd
Thermopolis WY 82443

Call Sign: W7KWR
William L Shields
130 Warren St
Thermopolis WY 82443

Call Sign: KA7MDW
Patricia K Maschke
Thermopolis WY 82443

Call Sign: KA7MOB
Robert M Maschke
Thermopolis WY 82443

Call Sign: KD7IDK
Calvin B Mccann
Thermopolis WY 82443

**FCC Amateur Radio
Licenses in Torrington**

Call Sign: WY7KVB
Kathy V Beaman
6881 A Rd 43
Torrington WY 822409116

Call Sign: N7ZFQ
Warren D Burgess
100 Antelope Ln
Torrington WY 82240

Call Sign: KC7SBL
Kelly J Cooper
123 Arrowhead Rd
Torrington WY 82240

Call Sign: W7WYO
High Plains Amateur
Radio Club
123 Arrowhead Rd
Torrington WY 82240

Call Sign: K7WY
Leroy Milner
123 Arrowhead Rd
Torrington WY 82240

Call Sign: KB7DZL
Beverly L Ericksen
3642 Big Horn
Torrington WY 82240

Call Sign: KB7TIP
Cristal L Ericksen
3642 Big Horn
Torrington WY 82240

Call Sign: KB7KU

Gregory A Ericksen
3642 Big Horn
Torrington WY 82240

Kathy V Beaman
Box 524
Torrington WY 822409116

Richard L Ackerson
208 E 29th Ave
Torrington WY 82240

Call Sign: N7XRM
Ross M Ericksen
3642 Big Horn
Torrington WY 82240

Call Sign: KE7ZGG
Richard S Oakley
4326 Buttermilk Rd
Torrington WY 82240

Call Sign: KA7KEW
Shelley J Ackerson
208 E 29th Ave
Torrington WY 82240

Call Sign: KA7DBY
Cora A Heyl
Box 173
Torrington WY 82240

Call Sign: N7EKI
Sue E Milner
111 Camino Del Rey
Torrington WY 82240

Call Sign: K7YPT
Wayne E Love
2317 E C St
Torrington WY 82240

Call Sign: KA7GOT
Rick A Shields
Box 269
Torrington WY 82240

Call Sign: K7CCD
Gary D Van Cleve
341 E 11th Ave
Torrington WY 82240

Call Sign: KD7KXH
George A Moore
2041 E C St Bsmt
Torrington WY 82240

Call Sign: KB7HNN
Kimberly K Des Enfants
Box 270
Torrington WY 82240

Call Sign: KA7DEZ
Rodney R Rutt
1603 E 20th Ave
Torrington WY 82240

Call Sign: WB7ABG
Donald L Spray
2702 E D St
Torrington WY 82240

Call Sign: N7DSV
Philip R Vanderpoel
Box 301A
Torrington WY 82240

Call Sign: KE7WWV
Richard L Nelson Jr
334 E 28th Ave
Torrington WY 82240

Call Sign: KD7PVJ
Les Austin
1618 E E St
Torrington WY 82240

Call Sign: KB7OYG
Christopher A Beaman
Box 524
Torrington WY 82240

Call Sign: KE7WWX
Spencer R Nelson
334 E 28th Ave
Torrington WY 82240

Call Sign: KD7JNQ
Kraig D Murphy
1601 E F 37
Torrington WY 82240

Call Sign: N7ZIG
Dale E Beaman Jr
Box 524
Torrington WY 82240

Call Sign: KA7KEZ
Patty L Vargas
208 E 29th Ave
Torrington WY 82240

Call Sign: W0DLL
Robert E Wiles
2133 E F St Apt D9
Torrington WY 822402521

Call Sign: KB7PYZ
Bradley A Beaman
Box 524
Torrington WY 82240

Call Sign: KC7TH
Carol J Ackerson
208 E 29th Ave
Torrington WY 82240

Call Sign: N7UHH
Debra R Wakamatsu
2415 E G St
Torrington WY 82240

Call Sign: KD7JJU

Call Sign: N7CG

Call Sign: N7CFR

Jon P Wakamatsu
2415 E G St
Torrington WY 82240

Call Sign: KC7SBK
Daniel C Marquez
1801 E J St
Torrington WY 822403131

Call Sign: KB7TIO
Rocky J Robbins
2542 Main St
Torrington WY 82240

Call Sign: N7GAC
Theodore C Steffens
7205 Rd 45V 7
Torrington WY 82240

Call Sign: KF7JPV
David L Muhlenkamp
4121 Rd 70L
Torrington WY 82240

Call Sign: KF7JPW
Sheila R Muhlenkamp
4121 Rd 70L
Torrington WY 82240

Call Sign: KF7BR
Donald L Rankin
4717 Rd 70Y
Torrington WY 82240

Call Sign: WA7OQI
Clifford N Moine
141 Rock Ridge Dr
Torrington WY 82240

Call Sign: WB7RGO
Dan A Ludwig
5058 St Hwy 161
Torrington WY 82240

Call Sign: K7STM

John B Patrick
11048 US Hwy 85
Torrington WY 82240

Call Sign: K7STM
The High Plains Contest
Club
11048 US Hwy 85
Torrington WY 82240

Call Sign: KF7GVM
The High Plains Contest
Club
11048 US Hwy 85
Torrington WY 82240

Call Sign: WK7K
John B Patrick
11048 US Hwy 85
Torrington WY 82240

Call Sign: WA7WXQ
Douglas N Des Enfants
5182 Van Tassell Rd
Torrington WY 82240

Call Sign: KB7OBD
Jordan D Marquez
1557 W B
Torrington WY 82240

Call Sign: KB7OBH
Henry A Mc Arthur
2825 W B
Torrington WY 82240

Call Sign: KC7AKK
Glen R Doren
1523 W C St
Torrington WY 82240

Call Sign: AD7IQ
Glen R Doren
1527 W C St
Torrington WY 82240

Call Sign: KD7LQX
Michael S Hofer
1549 W C St
Torrington WY 82240

Call Sign: KB7NZU
Kenneth G Hoff
Torrington WY 82240

Call Sign: KD7OXV
Doug J Butler
Torrington WY 82240

Call Sign: WA7ALI
Robert D Heyl
Torrington WY 82240

Call Sign: WB0PRN
Norman P Mac Intosh
Torrington WY 82240

Call Sign: KK7UE
Eric D Stephenson
Torrington WY 82240

**FCC Amateur Radio
Licenses in Upton**

Call Sign: W7NMW
Harry E Clingan
1215 Pearl St
Upton WY 82730

Call Sign: WA7WAE
Bobby J Davis
1508 Pine St
Upton WY 82730

Call Sign: KE7HMK
Alan L Todd
Upton WY 82730

Call Sign: W7TE
Alan L Todd

Upton WY 82730

FCC Amateur Radio Licenses in Wamsutter

Call Sign: KE7LBB
Michael D Carter
Wamsutter WY 82336

FCC Amateur Radio Licenses in Wapiti

Call Sign: KB1FTI
Andrew V Balkus
Wapiti WY 82450

Call Sign: N7SYE
James L Gallagher
Wapiti WY 82450

Call Sign: KF7MC
Mary E Williams
Wapiti WY 82450

Call Sign: N7LKH
Robert W Williams
Wapiti WY 82450

Call Sign: KF7UIJ
Allen Clow
Wapiti WY 82450

Call Sign: KE7UJB
Martin M Moon
Wapiti WY 82450

FCC Amateur Radio Licenses in Weston

Call Sign: KE7NBF
Chris G Bliss
1107 Parks Rd
Weston WY 82731

Call Sign: K7WIZ

Franklin E Bliss
1107 Parks Rd
Weston WY 82731

Call Sign: KE7NBG
Franklin E Bliss
1107 Parks Rd
Weston WY 82731

FCC Amateur Radio Licenses in Wheatland

Call Sign: N7UCL
Clifford L Flaharty
303 13th St
Wheatland WY 82201

Call Sign: AE7LN
Leonard C Noyce
903 16th St
Wheatland WY 82201

Call Sign: KE7VIC
Leonard C Noyce
903 16th St
Wheatland WY 82201

Call Sign: KB7DUQ
Floyd E Rhoades
302 20th
Wheatland WY 82201

Call Sign: KB7DUP
David C Rhoades
302 20th St
Wheatland WY 82201

Call Sign: KA7SGQ
Clayton L Jons
87 Antelope Gap Rd
Wheatland WY 82201

Call Sign: KC7II
Richard O Anshutz
Box 174

Wheatland WY 82201

Call Sign: KF7RNG
Cliff A Bennett
1150 Cedar St
Wheatland WY 822012637

Call Sign: KD7UGW
Max M Carter
56 Cozad Rd
Wheatland WY 82201

Call Sign: KC7KJU
Gale O Rutherford
49 Dwyer Rd
Wheatland WY 82201

Call Sign: KD7ADE
Silvia B Rutherford
49 Dwyer Rd
Wheatland WY 82201

Call Sign: W7TQU
Darrel D Vogt
224 E Oak
Wheatland WY 82201

Call Sign: KF7SAV
Leslie T Atkinson
73 Ferguson Rd
Wheatland WY 82201

Call Sign: KB7UGM
Harvey O Hoeck
11 Fern Dr
Wheatland WY 82201

Call Sign: W7HAP
Robert A Rice
41 Gibson Rd
Wheatland WY 82201

Call Sign: WA7NLV
Michael R Rice
65 Gibson Rd

Wheatland WY 82201

Call Sign: KC2NZ
James S Anderson
381 Goodrich Rd
Wheatland WY 82201

Call Sign: N2IEZ
Sandra Eliz K Anderson
381 Goodrich Rd
Wheatland WY 82201

Call Sign: AE7AF
James S Anderson
381 Goodrich Rd
Wheatland WY 82201

Call Sign: KC7FVM
James T Hedstrom
1176 Hightower
Wheatland WY 82201

Call Sign: N7OTY
Larry D Elling
1216 Hightower
Wheatland WY 82201

Call Sign: N7HRO
Dennis L Cornell
119 Hightower Rd
Wheatland WY 82201

Call Sign: K7UWR
Larry O Dean
1763 Hwy 34
Wheatland WY 82201

Call Sign: WA7JIJ
Frances M Laganiere
15 Loretta Dr
Wheatland WY 82201

Call Sign: WA7DFK
Raoul A Laganiere
15 Loretta Dr

Wheatland WY 82201

Call Sign: KC7KJR
Anne M Brickman
438 N Dwyer Rd
Wheatland WY 82201

Call Sign: KC7KJS
Douglas L Brickman
438 N Dwyer Rd
Wheatland WY 82201

Call Sign: KA0INI
John E Bell
299 N Wheatland Hwy
Wheatland WY 82201

Call Sign: N0NNG
William B Wales
229 Olson Rd
Wheatland WY 82201

Call Sign: WA7SNU
Terry T Meier
208 Park Ave
Wheatland WY 82201

Call Sign: K1BM
Bob Margolin
Wheatland WY 82201

Call Sign: KM5HV
Matthan A Stafford Jr
Wheatland WY 82201

FCC Amateur Radio Licenses in Wilson

Call Sign: KF7GCI
Rheim B Jones
3475 Box Elder Pl
Wilson WY 83014

Call Sign: KF7QEV
Joseph G Piccoli

3625 Cheney Ln
Wilson WY 83014

Call Sign: N6YEY
Tiki Mashy
3465 N Pines Way 104
Wilson WY 83014

Call Sign: W6KGP
Leonard J Kleiman
2075 No Moose Wilson Rd
Wilson WY 830141148

Call Sign: KC7WZK
Larry Detrick
Wilson WY 83014

Call Sign: KD7QWO
John M Scott
Wilson WY 83014

Call Sign: N1UAQ
Manuel Wenger
Wilson WY 830141568

Call Sign: KC7BDZ
Robert I Womble
Wilson WY 83014

Call Sign: KE7DJZ
Hugh S Owens
Wilson WY 83014

Call Sign: KE7DJY
Karlene L Owens
Wilson WY 83014

Call Sign: KE7FIO
Peter C Mackay
Wilson WY 83014

FCC Amateur Radio Licenses in Wolf

Call Sign: KE7OMM

Brian R Pearce
1026 Soldier Creek Rd
Wolf WY 82844

FCC Amateur Radio Licenses in Worland

Call Sign: KF7KHK
Terry A Sutherland
1301 Airport Rd
Worland WY 82401

Call Sign: K7SAR
Douglas Sothan
1410 Charles Ave
Worland WY 82401

Call Sign: KD7HH
Roger W Barnhill Sr
213 Chukar Dr
Worland WY 82401

Call Sign: KD7HI
Belinda L Barnhill
213 Chukar Dr
Worland WY 82401

Call Sign: KC7LQD
Roger H Howe
1601 Circle Rd
Worland WY 82401

Call Sign: KF7BJO
Bernard M Swalstad
1900 Cloud Peak Dr Apt 1
Worland WY 82401

Call Sign: KF7RB
Adolph J Shorte
1004 Coburn Ave
Worland WY 82401

Call Sign: WA7CGK
Stanton J Abell Jr
3012 Columbine

Worland WY 82401

Call Sign: KE7UUY
Kimball R Croft
107 Country Dr
Worland WY 82401

Call Sign: KF7PHA
Edward D Zimmerman
313 Hillcrest
Worland WY 82401

Call Sign: WB0VQI
Charles O Fritz Jr
716 Hwy 433
Worland WY 82401

Call Sign: WB7RYH
Charles O Fritz Sr
716 Hwy 433
Worland WY 82401

Call Sign: WB7RYI
Naomi E Fritz
716 Hwy 433
Worland WY 82401

Call Sign: KI7W
Big Horn Basin Amateur
Radio Club
771 Hwy 433 N
Worland WY 82401

Call Sign: W7PN
Karl E Prinsen Sr
771 Hwy 433 N
Worland WY 82401

Call Sign: WY7YL
Lani Underwood
1404 Lane 17
Worland WY 82401

Call Sign: KE7YIR
Kathryn Q Mulkey

421 N 8th St Apt 4
Worland WY 82401

Call Sign: N7GDY
Bonnetta M Wray
1212 Pulliam Ave
Worland WY 824012830

Call Sign: W0RAY
Calvin E Wray
1212 Pulliam Ave
Worland WY 82401

Call Sign: KD7VP
Calvin E Wray
1212 Pulliam Ave
Worland WY 824012830

Call Sign: KK7WO
Calvin E Wray
1212 Pulliam Ave
Worland WY 824012830

Call Sign: KB7PLA
Kenneth T Brown
1001 Rd 10
Worland WY 824011076

Call Sign: AB7VK
Gerald C White
401 Rd 11 S
Worland WY 82401

Call Sign: KE7UUZ
Lucy J Leyva
801 S 10th St
Worland WY 82401

Call Sign: K0GHT
David M Lechelt
816 S 10th St
Worland WY 82401

Call Sign: KF7PGZ
David M Lechelt

816 S 10th St
Worland WY 82401

Call Sign: KB1SBI
Nathaniel V Beckman
206 S 11th St
Worland WY 82401

Call Sign: N7OHG
Bill D Kumpe
320 S 12th
Worland WY 82401

Call Sign: KF7MVR
Kyle J Weaver
713 S 13th
Worland WY 82401

Call Sign: KF7STN
Kim A Barr
408 S 18th
Worland WY 82401

Call Sign: KF7STM
Kari A Barr
408 S 18th St
Worland WY 82401

Call Sign: K7SGF
Grover T Briggs
305 S 22
Worland WY 82401

Call Sign: KC7GKV
George E Easton
201 S 5th St
Worland WY 82401

Call Sign: KF7GHX
Taylor Y Ulman
2162 S Flat Rd
Worland WY 82401

Call Sign: KA7DGD
Freddie L Geiser

1308 S Flat Village
Worland WY 82401

Call Sign: N5AGE
Armando Nunez
1216 S Ln
Worland WY 82401

Call Sign: KD0LPJ
Vickie D Nunez
1216 S Ln
Worland WY 82401

Call Sign: AD7XI
Michael W Donnell
411 Sagebrush Dr
Worland WY 82401

Call Sign: KE7UVA
Michael W Donnell
411 Sagebrush Dr
Worland WY 82401

Call Sign: KF7TN
Gene J Leone
660 Sunnyside Ln
Worland WY 82401

Call Sign: KM5KS
John W Sinclair
800 Swan Place
Worland WY 82401

Call Sign: AE7FR
John W Sinclair
800 Swan Place
Worland WY 82401

Call Sign: WY7JS
John W Sinclair
800 Swan Place
Worland WY 82401

Call Sign: KE7YIS
Herman L Stayman

516 Teton Pl
Worland WY 82401

Call Sign: KC7EMT
Donald D Voyles
613 Thomas Ave
Worland WY 82401

Call Sign: K7GBX
Raymond W Harrison Jr
170 W River Rd
Worland WY 82401

Call Sign: K7ETE
Curt L Evans
Worland WY 82401

FCC Amateur Radio Licenses in Wright

Call Sign: KC8JOR
Michael A Phipps
303 Shadow Hill Ln
Wright WY 82732

Call Sign: KB7IXE
Delbert R Barber
Wright WY 827320043

FCC Amateur Radio Licenses in Yellowstone National Park

Call Sign: KB7IIX
Clarence H Coleman
Yellowstone National Park
WY 82190

Call Sign: KC7NVG
Jeffrey D Voyles
Yellowstone National Park
WY 82190